The Apocalypse of St. John

Rev. E. Sylvester Berry

First published by John H. Winterich in 1921.

Copyright © Rev. E. Sylvester Berry.

This edition published in 2016.

Table of Contents

PREFACE

The book of the Apocalypse is unlike any other book of the New Testament — and is full of consolation and instruction to all who read its inspired and prophetic words. It lifts the soul up to the beauty and grandeur of Heaven — shows us in all their glory the joys and triumphs of those who were once like ourselves — but who are now changed and happy with those "who have washed their robes and made them white in the blood of the Lamb." How consoling it is to turn from the sordid things of earth — to be carried away with the sublime words that lead us to the throne of God — to the company of the Angels and Saints — to the new Jerusalem with streets of gold — to the river and tree of life — to hear the voice of God Himself saying "Blessed is he that keepeth the words of the prophecy of this book."

The following pages will be most interesting to those who love to study the word of God. Father Berry has entered a new field — for there is practically no study of the Apocalypse in the English language — and the points and explanations he has placed before us are both interesting and instructive. The student will read it with pleasure and profit. St. Jerome tells us "The Apocalypse has as many mysteries as words — or rather mysteries in every word." The author has tried in a simple scholarly way to help us view them all with pleasure and understanding.

JAMES J. HARTLEY,
Bishop of Columbus.
Columbus, Ohio, June 18th, 1921.

INTRODUCTION

In the study of Holy Scripture it is necessary to bear in mind that its various books are not separate and independent works. It is true, they were written by persons widely distant from one another in time and place, yet the Holy Ghost, their true Author, coordinates them all to one common purpose. The different books are but so many chapters of one and the same great work whose first chapter recounts the origin of the world by creation; its last, foretells the final consummation of all things. The intervening chapters relate in order various happenings between these two extremes.

The Bible does not give a complete history of mankind; in fact it is not intended to teach history as such. The Holy Ghost wishes to strengthen our faith, arouse our hopes in the mercies of God, and instill our hearts with the fear of His punishments. For this purpose He gives a summary view of God's dealings with mankind. There is only an occasional glimpse of things not closely connected with this main purpose. The origin of the material world is briefly sketched while the creation of the angels is only referred to incidentally. But the questions which concern us more directly are treated at length. Our nature, our origin, and our destiny summarize the content of Holy Scripture. It teaches that man is a free and intelligent being created in a state of grace and destined to be united with God in Heaven for all eternity. Through abuse of free will man fell from this high estate and is daily exposed to sin and suffering, but the merits of Christ's death on the cross have redeemed man's fallen nature and placed him once more upon the way of salvation.

The person of Christ thus becomes the central figure of all Scripture. He is the alpha and omega, the beginning and the end."[1] As God, He created all things "and without Him was made nothing that was made. In Him was life and the life was the light of men."[2] As man, Christ is the greatest handiwork of God, the "first-born of every creature:"[3] As the God-man, He is our Redeemer, the "only name under Heaven given to men whereby we

---

[1] Apocalypse i, 8.

[2] St. John i, 3, 4.

[3] Colossians i, 15.

must be saved."[4] Thus is Jesus Christ the center from which all things radiate, around which all revolve, and in which all must finally converge.

After recounting the creation and fall of man, the Old Testament announces the coming of the Savior and narrates the preparation of mankind for this great event. The Gospels and Epistles give the life of our Lord and rehearse His teachings. The Acts of the Apostles outline the first years of the new-born Church. The Apocalypse gives a prophetic history of the Church from the days of St. John to the final consummation of the world.

In its general purpose the Apocalypse does not differ from the other Scriptures. It is to teach men a knowledge of God, enlighten their faith, strengthen their hopes, and give them a rule of conduct by which they may obtain eternal salvation. It is also intended to fortify the faithful in time of trial and temptation, and to guide the Church in every age. In this respect the Apocalypse simply enlarges upon the warnings of Christ concerning persecution of His Church. "The servant is not greater than his master. If they persecuted me they will also persecute you. . . . They will put you out of the synagogue; yea the hour cometh that whosoever killeth you, will think that he doth a service to God."[5] Christ has promised that the gates of hell shall never prevail against His Church,[6] but this very promise foreshadows a mighty conflict with the powers of darkness. The Apocalypse tells of the trials and sufferings of the Church in this great conflict and prophesies her final triumph according to the promise of Christ: "Behold I am with you all days even to the consummation of the world."[7] Hence the prophecies of the Apocalypse should be a source of consolation when we see the Church opposed and persecuted for we have the assurance of the Holy Ghost that she shall come forth triumphant and reign peacefully over all nations.

In other parts of Scripture, purely historical events serve merely as a background upon which are depicted the designs of Providence. St. John pursues a similar method in the Apocalypse. He does not intend to give a detailed prophetic history of the Church. He singles out the more important points to serve as guide-posts along the course of centuries. It may be said

---

[4] Acts of the Apostles iv, 12.

[5] St. John xv, 18-20; xvi, 2.

[6] St. Matthew xvi, 18.

[7] St. Matthew xxviii, 20.

that he gives only the philosophy of the Church's history, — the underlying causes of all its outward events.

The laws of sacred and profane history are alike; similar causes must produce similar effects. Hence all history repeats itself in general outlines. Only accidental circumstances differ. This explains why the Apocalypse is written under the form of symbolic visions instead of ordinary discourse. It must give in a few pages a resume of many centuries. One and the same prophecy often announces many similar events separated in time by centuries. The account must be limited to the barest outlines and stripped of every accidental circumstance. Symbolic visions are best suited to this purpose. Moreover they admit of mystic and moral interpretations profitable to the faithful of every age.

The prophecies of the Apocalypse consist almost entirely of symbolic visions whose allegorical sense must be the sense intended by the Holy Ghost. Any other interpretation is unwarranted except where the Apostle has evidently abandoned allegory for ordinary discourse. The chief duty of the interpreter is to search out the key of each symbol. The prophetic writings of the Old Testament greatly facilitate this work because the Apocalypse is strongly tinged with the imagery of the prophets of old and in many instances it further develops prophecies first announced by them.

A study of the Gospels and Epistles also gives a clue to the proper interpretation of many things in the Apocalypse. Thus, for example, the Gospels make it plain that the kingdom of God" or the "kingdom of Heaven" is the Church in time or in eternity. Again it is evident from the Epistles and from the Acts of the Apostles that the "ancients" are the Apostles, and the bishops and priests of the church.[8]

In some cases St. John himself gives the key to his visions. Thus, an angel is an Apostle or bishop sent by Christ to teach and govern His Church. In a similar sense our Lord calls St. John the Baptist an "angel."[9] In other cases the meaning is evident from the context. The "Lamb standing as it were slain"[10] can be none other than Christ triumphant at the right hand of God the Father. Hence the words "as it were slain" must refer to Christ mystically slain in the Holy Eucharist.

---

[8] Cf. Acts xi, 30; xiv, 23; Titus i, 5; 1 Timothy v. 19; 1 Peter v. 1.

[9] St. Matthew xi, 10.

[10] Apocalypse v, 6.

It has been customary to divide the Apocalypse into seven visions with a prologue and an epilogue, as follows:

Prologue I, 1-8

1st Vision. — Letters to the seven churches. 1, 9 — iii, 22.

2nd Vision. — The seven seals, iv, 1 — viii, 1.

3rd Vision — The seven trumpets, viii, 2 — xi, 18.

4th Vision. — (a) The woman and the dragon.

(b) The beast of the sea.

(c) The beast of the earth.

(d) The harvest and the vintage, xi, 19 — xiv, 8.

5th Vision. — The seven angels with seven plagues, xv, 1— xix, 21.

6th Vision. — The binding and loosing of Satan, xx, 1-15.

7th Vision. — The resurrection, general judgment, and the heavenly Jerusalem, xxi, 1 — xxii, 5.

Epilogue XXII, 6-21

Instead of this commonly received division,[11] the following is here submitted in the belief that it is justified by the commentary which follows. Yet in this, as in all things, we submit to the unerring judgment of the Church, the "pillar and ground of the truth."[12]

Prologue I, 1-8

Part I

From the Days of St. John to the Opening of the Abyss

i. — General warning to the churches, i, 9 — iii, 22.

ii. — Constitution of the Church, chs. iv-v.

iii. — Persecution of the Church, and fall of the pagan Empire of Rome. ch. vi.

iv. — The Church firmly established, ch. vii.

V. — The Vicissitudes of the Church, ch. viii.

Part II

From the Opening of the Abyss to its Closing

i. — Preparation for the Reign of Antichrist.

---

[11] Cf. Cornely, "Cursus Scripturae Sacra e" vol. iii, page 715 sq.; Gigot, "Apocalypse of St. John" in Westminster version.

[12] 1 Timothy iii, 15.

(a) Heresies and Religious Wars. ch. ix.

(b) A Preparatory Vision, ch. x.

(c) The Two Witnesses. ch. xi.

(d) Conflict between the Church and Satan, ch. xii.

ii. — The Reign of Antichrist and his Overthrow.

(a) Antichrist and his Prophet, ch. xiii.

(b) Prophets of Victory, ch. xiv.

(c) Seven Plagues on the Empire of Antichrist, chs. xv-xvi.

(d) The Beast and the Harlot, ch. xvii.

(e) The Fall of Babylon, ch. xviii.

(f) The Hymn of Victory, and the Condemnation of Antichrist and his Prophet, ch. xix.

Part III

From the Closing of the Abyss to the End of the World

i. — The Universal Reign of Jesus Christ, xx, 1-6.

ii. — The Loosing of Satan and the Last Persecution, xx, 7-10.

iii. — The Resurrection and General Judgment, xx, 11-15.

iv. — The Heavenly Jerusalem, xxi, 1 — xxii, 5.

Epilogue XX, 6-20

According to this division the three parts of the Apocalypse correspond to three successive periods in the history of the Church and furnish a prophetic history that extends from the time of St. John to the final triumph of the Church in glory.

The above division of the Apocalypse and the explanation which follows are based upon an article by Pere Gallois, O. P., which first appeared in the Revue Biblique. It was then issued in pamphlet form by P. Lethielleux, Paris, in 1895, with a prefatory letter by Pere Monsabre, O. P., which, we believe, is sufficient guaranty for its complete orthodoxy. The present work is practically an enlarged adaptation of the article by Pere Gallois, but many departures from his opinions demand that it be issued as a separate work with due acknowledgment to the original author. It is not intended to be a complete exegesis of the Apocalypse, yet we hope it may lead to a better understanding of those obscure prophecies in which the Holy Ghost foretells the vicissitudes of the Church and its final triumph over all enemies.

THE PROLOGUE

Blessed is he that readeth and heareth the words of this prophecy; and keepeth those things which are written in it.

APOCALYPSE
iv: i.

THE PROLOGUE

CHAPTER I

1. The revelation of Jesus Christ, which God gave unto him, to make known to his servants the things which must shortly come to pass and signified, sending by his angel to his servant John, 2 who hath given testimony to the word of God, and the testimony of Jesus Christ, what things soever he hath seen.

3. Blessed is he that readeth and heareth the words of this prophecy: and keepeth those things which are written in it. For the time is at hand.

1. The revelation (apocalypse) of Jesus Christ. The Greek word αποκάλυψη signifies a revelation; a making known. It also means the revealing of one's self, a coming. Both meanings are appropriate here. It is a revelation which Christ has made concerning His Coming in power and majesty. It is also a prophecy of events leading up to this second coming.

These things "must shortly come to pass." They comprise the whole history of the Church from the time of Christ until the end of the world. Hence their accomplishment was already beginning in the days of St. John.

This revelation has been confided to Jesus Christ by God the Father. Christ in turn sends an angel to impart it to His servant John. Angels are the natural intermediaries between God and man. They often fulfilled this mission before the time of Christ. Today their ministry is less needed for this purpose since we have the unerring Church of Christ as our teacher and guide in all things pertaining to salvation.

2. By writing these revelations St. John has given testimony to God and to Jesus Christ. Testimony may be given by word or by works, especially by martyrdom. St. John here gives testimony by written word.

3. Whoever reads this book, opens his heart to its teachings, and conforms his life to its precepts is worthy of eternal happiness. Let no one say that the book was written for future ages only. It is already being fulfilled and every Christian should find therein a rule of life suited to the circumstances in which God has placed him.

CHAPTER I

4. John to the seven churches which are in Asia. Grace be to you and peace from him that is, and that was, and that is to come, and from the seven spirits which are before his throne.

5. And from Jesus Christ, who is the faithful witness, the first begotten of the dead, and the prince of the kings of the earth, who hath loved us, and washed us from our sins in his own blood, 6, and hath made us a kingdom and priests to God and his Father, to him be glory and empire for ever and ever. Amen.

7. Behold he cometh with the clouds, and every eye shall see him, and they also that pierced him. And all tribes of earth shall bewail themselves because of him. Even so. Amen.

8. I am alpha and omega, the beginning and the end, saith the Lord God, who is, and who was, and who is to come, the Almighty.

4. St. John begins by laying down a rule of conduct for those of his own times. He is an Apostle, and in particular, the Apostle of Asia Minor. Hence he addresses himself to the bishops and churches of that province; yet his words are of universal application. Through the churches of Asia Minor, he addresses all churches throughout the world for all time.

Some interpreters take the seven churches as types of seven ages in the Church. Much can be said in favor of this opinion, but it is difficult to distinguish periods in the Church corresponding to the characteristics of these seven churches as described in the Apocalypse. Thus, for example, the church of Ephesus, characterized by lack of fervor and zeal, would represent the Apostolic period of the Church. But it cannot be said with any historical accuracy that the Church in that age was especially noted for lack of fervor and zeal.

The simpler and, as we believe, the more correct view likens these letters of St. John to many of St. Paul's Epistles which were written to particular churches for particular purposes, but intended by the Holy Ghost to be documents of warning and instruction for all churches and for all times. The universal character is much more evident in these seven letters than in the Epistles of St. Paul. They were not sent as separate letters to the individual churches, but form an integral part of the Apocalypse which was sent to each church as one complete document.

In Holy Scripture "seven" is the most sacred of numbers. The seventh day of the week was consecrated to God in a special manner. The Paschal feast lasted seven days. Seven weeks later came the feast of Pentecost when seven lambs were offered in sacrifice. Seven sprinklings of blood were prescribed for sin. In the Holy Place stood the seven-branched candlestick with its seven lights. In fact the number seven is found on almost every page of Holy Scripture. It is the perfect number, the symbol of perfection, fullness, or universality. It seems to have acquired this meaning from the fact that God completed the work of creation in six days and rested on the seventh which He blessed and sanctified.[13]

The Apostle prays for peace and grace; not such peace as the world can give, but peace and grace from God. "Peace I leave with you; my peace I give unto you; not as the world giveth, do I give unto you."[14] This peace from heaven is proclaimed upon earth by the seven spirits who stand before the throne of God. Three of them are known by name. They are the Archangels Raphael, Gabriel, and Michael. St. Raphael said: "I am the Angel Raphael, one of the seven, who stand before the Lord." He was sent with a message of peace to Tobias of old.[15] St. Gabriel announced peace to Daniel, to the Priest Zacharias, and to the Blessed Virgin.[16] St. Michael, the special protector of the Jewish nation,[17] now guards the Church against her enemies that she too, may enjoy the peace that comes from God.[18]

5. The seven spirits also represent the ministers of the Church who preach the Gospel of peace and grace to all nations. Jesus Christ, their Master, is the Prince of Peace, and becomes for us the source of all grace through the merits of His life, death and resurrection. All earthly kings and rulers must accept His law and govern according to His precepts because He is King of kings and Lord of lords.

Through the infinite love of Jesus Christ we have been redeemed and cleansed from sin by His Blood. "Having loved his own who were in the world, he loved them unto the end."[19] "And the blood of Jesus Christ cleanseth us from all sin."[20]

---

[13] Genesis ii, 1-3.

[14] St. John xiv, 27.

[15] Tobias xii. 15.

[16] Daniel ix, 21; St. Luke i, 19-26.

[17] Daniel xii, 1.

[18] Apocalypse xii, 7.

[19] St. John xiii, 1.

[20] 1 John i, 7.

6. Christ has established the Church as His kingdom upon earth with the bishops and priests as its teachers and rulers. Hence St. John says to the bishops, his co-laborers in the Church: We have been made kings and co-heirs of His kingdom; we have been chosen priests to render glory to His eternal Father. To Christ also belongs equal honor through all ages because he is God, equal to the Father in all things.

Those to whom St. John writes are priests and rulers in the Church. This proves that St. John does not write directly to the different churches but to their bishops. Hence the words of praise or reproof written to the "angels" are personal warnings to the bishops and through them to the churches.

7. Looking down the vista of ages, St. John sees our Lord coming in clouds of glory to judge the living and the dead. With the prophets of old, clouds were ever symbols of divine majesty. It is worthy of note that the Apocalypse is literally filled with striking expressions of St. John's faith in the divinity of Christ. This is proof sufficient that this dogma of Faith was not invented after the time of the Apostles as rationalists would have us believe.

At His second coming Christ will be manifest to all; even those who put Him to death on the cross shall behold His power and majesty. Then will all nations mourn because of the judgment that awaits them. The last words of this verse express the certainty that these things must come to pass. They are also a prayer: "So let it be. Amen."

8. Alpha is the first letter of the Greek alphabet, and omega the last. Hence Christ calls Himself "alpha and omega, the beginning and the end."

PART I: From the Time of Christ to the Opening of the Abyss

The voice which I heard, as it were the voice of a trumpet said: Come up hither, and I will show thee the things which must be done hereafter.

APOCALYPSE
iv: 1.

GENERAL WARNING TO THE CHURCHES

9. I John, your brother and your partner in tribulation, and in the kingdom, and patience in Christ Jesus, was in the island which is called Patmos, for the word of God and for the testimony of Jesus.

10. I was in the spirit on the Lord's day, and heard behind me a great voice, as of a trumpet,

11. Saying: What thou seest, write in a book: and send to the seven churches which are in Asia, to Ephesus, and to Smyrna, and to Pergamus, and to Thyatira, and to Sardis and to Philadelphia, and to Laodicea.

12. And I turned to see the voice that spoke with me. And being turned, I saw seven golden candlesticks:

13. And in the midst of the seven golden candlesticks, one like to the son of man, clothed with a garment down to the feet, and girt about the paps with a golden girdle.

14. And his head and his hairs were white, as white wool, and as snow, and his eyes were as a flame of fire.

15. And his feet were like unto fine brass, as in a burning furnace. And his voice as the sound of many waters.

16. And he had in his right hand seven stars. And from his mouth came out a sharp two-edged sword: and his face was as the sun shineth in his power.

17. And when I had seen him, I fell at his feet as dead. And he laid his right hand upon me, saying: Fear not. I am the first and the last,

18. And alive and was dead, and behold I am living for ever and ever and have the keys of death and of hell.

19. Write therefore the things which thou hast seen, and which are and which must be done hereafter.

20. The mystery of the seven stars, which thou sawest in my right hand and the seven golden candlesticks. The seven stars are the seven angels of the seven churches. And the seven candlesticks are the seven churches.

9. "For the word of God and for the testimony of Jesus" refers to sufferings which St. John endured for his faith. Thus the martyrs were slain "for the word of God, and for the testimony which they held."[21] This

interpretation is confirmed by the fact that the Apostle shared in the sufferings of his brethren; he was "a partner in their tribulations." He was even then suffering the hardships of exile in Patmos.

Many authors take the words of St. John to mean that he was on the Island of Patmos for the purpose of receiving the "word of God" and to give testimony by his writing. But in the Apocalypse St. John does not use the Greek word "dia" in connection with the "word of God" to express a purpose. It always means "for the sake of" or "in consequence of." No doubt, St. John would also look upon his banishment as an act of divine Providence preparing him for these great revelations.

Toward the end of Domitian's reign, St. John was brought to Rome and cast into a cauldron of boiling oil. Miraculously escaping from this he was banished to the Island of Patmos about the year 95 A. D.[22] Upon the death of Domitian the following year, St. John returned to Ephesus where he died a peaceful death about 100 A. D.

Patmos is a desolate island of volcanic rocks in the Aegean Sea, about sixty miles southwest of Ephesus. Its excellent harbor made it a stopping place for vessels on the way from Rome to Ephesus. Pliny informs us that it was used as a place of exile.[23] A cave about half way between the shore and the modern town of Patmos is pointed out as the spot where St. John received his revelations.

10. St. John received this revelation on Sunday — the Lord's day. This fact is interesting because it shows at what an early date the Christians dedicated the first day of the week to the service of God as indicated by the name Lord's day.[24] Perhaps St. John had withdrawn from his fellow exiles on that day to devote himself to prayer. While thus engaged in prayer he heard a voice clear and piercing as a trumpet blast. It was a voice to be heard to the uttermost parts of the earth.

12, 13. Turning to see whence the voice came, St. John beheld a vision of seven golden candlesticks, and in the midst of them our Lord, clothed in the white robe of the priesthood. He appeared to St. John in his human form — "like to the son of man."

---

[21] Apocalypse vi, 9.

[22] Eusebius, "Church History" iii, 18; Tertullian, "Prescriptions against Heretics" xxxvi.

[23] Pliny, "Natural History" iv, 12,13.

[24] Cf. also Acts of the Apostles xx, 7; 1 Corinthians xvi, 2.

The seven candlesticks represent the seven churches of Asia. As noted above, seven is the perfect number which denotes universality. Hence by extension the seven candlesticks represent all churches throughout the world for all time. Gold signifies the charity of Christ which pervades and vivifies the Church.

14. The snow-white locks are a symbol of wisdom and eternity. The all-seeing eyes were as flames of fire — terrible to the wicked, but a symbol of all-consuming love for the faithful. Fire is one of God's great gifts to man, yet it is also man's most destructive enemy.

15. The feet of glowing brass remind us of the rigorous justice of divine judgments. The voice, like the roar of mighty waters, proclaims mercy and love to the faithful, but threatens punishment to the wicked. Water, like fire, is a great good, or a terrible evil according to circumstances.

16. The seven stars represent the seven bishops of Asia and through them all bishops of the Church. Bishops are stars set in the firmament of the Church to enlighten and direct the faithful through the dark sea of life. Christ holds the stars in His right hand to show His great solicitude for those charged with the government of His Church and the care of souls.

The sharp two-edged sword is the Gospel which destroys sin and heresy. "The word of God is living and effectual, and more piercing than any two-edged sword."[25] The countenance, bright as noon-day sun, reveals the glory of Christ's risen body. It is also a symbol of the enlightening power of the Gospel which leaves the wicked without excuse for their willful blindness. "If I had not come and spoken to them, they would not have sin: but now they have no excuse for their sin."[26]

17, 18. Overcome with fear and admiration St. John fell to the ground. Our Lord then revealed His identity with words of reassurance: "Fear not, for I am the Lord who arose from the dead to die no more." "Christ rising again from the dead, dieth now no more; death shall no more have dominion over him"[27] because He holds the keys of death and hell. The words of Christ must certainly have carried St. John back to that other scene on Mount Tabor where our Lord revealed His glory to the three Apostles some sixty-five years before.[28]

---

[25] Hebrews iv, 12.

[26] St. John xv, 22.

[27] Romans vi, 9.

[28] St. Matthew xvii, 1-8.

19, 20. Christ Himself explains the meaning of the candlesticks and stars. He thus shows that the prophecies of the Apocalypse are to be understood in an allegorical sense unless the text clearly indicates a different interpretation. In some few passages the meaning is explained. In most cases the interpretation must be sought in the writings of the prophets who used like symbols to express similar truths.

TO THE CHURCH OF EPHESUS

CHAPTER II

1. Unto the angel of the church of Ephesus write: These things saith he, who holdeth the seven stars in his right hand, who walketh in the midst of the seven golden candlesticks:

2. I know thy work, and thy labor, and thy patience, and how thou canst not bear them that are evil, and thou hast tried them who say they are apostles, are not, and hast found them liars;

3. And thou hast patience, and hast endured for my name and hast not fainted.

4. But I have somewhat against thee, because thou hast left thy first charity.

5. Be mindful therefore from whence thou art fallen: and do penance, and do thy first works. Or else I will come to thee, and will move thy candlestick out of its place, except thou do penance.

6. But this thou hast, that thou hatest the deeds of the Nicolaites, which I also hate.

7. He that hath an ear, let him hear what the spirit saith to the churches. To him that overcometh, I will give to eat of the tree of life, which is in the paradise of my God.

1. The angels addressed by St. John are the bishops of the churches to which he writes. The Greek word αγγελος means "one sent," a "messenger." Bishops are ministers sent by Christ to rule His Church. Ephesus was an important city on the western coast of Asia Minor. It was chiefly noted for the temple of Diana which was counted among the seven wonders of the world. The temple was stripped of its riches by Nero and finally destroyed by the Goths in 262 A. D. St. Paul preached the Gospel in Ephesus for three years and left his disciple, St. Timothy, as bishop, to carry on the work. St. John also spent his last years at Ephesus where he wrote the fourth Gospel. An ancient tradition says that Mary Magdalene also died at Ephesus.

Today Ephesus is represented by Aya Solouk, a village of 3000 inhabitants. Below the village lie the ruins of the ancient city. Remains of the temple and theater are still pointed out to the visitor.

St. Timothy was probably the "angel" of Ephesus to whom St. John writes in the Apocalypse. He is praised for his untiring labors in preaching the Gospel and his zeal in rooting out false teachers. He has also suffered persecution for Christ's name. St. Paul informs us that St. Timothy had been imprisoned for his faith, but he gives none of the circumstances.[29]

St. Timothy is now reprimanded because he has lost much of his former zeal. St. Paul had recognized in his beloved disciple a gentleness of nature that easily leads to the lack of that zeal and firmness so necessary in a bishop. Hence he wrote to St. Timothy: "Stir up the grace of God which is in thee by the imposition of my hands. For God hath not given us the spirit of fear; but of power, and of love, and of sobriety." And again: "Preach the word. Be instant in season and out of season. Reprove, entreat, rebuke in all patience and doctrine."[30]

What St. Paul feared has come to pass. The words of St. John leave the impression that there has been a serious falling off in fervor and zeal. The consequences will be all the greater now that persecution is at hand. St. John takes the place of the former master to warn St. Timothy. His words were fruitful and St. Timothy won the martyr's crown soon after.

To persevere in fervor and zeal is one of the greatest difficulties of an apostolic life. Yet it is the strict duty of every apostle worthy the name.

5. A terrible punishment awaits St. Timothy unless he regain his former zeal in the ministry. The nature of this chastisement indicates that the faithful were at fault even more than their bishop. "I will remove thy candlestick (church) out of its place" by means of persecution, heresy, schism, and apostasy. Only too often has this threat been carried out in the history of the Church. It is a menace hanging over every church that loses its first fervor and abandons its first works.

6. Our Lord commends St. Timothy for his hatred of the Nicolaite heresy. The Nicolaites were noted for their corrupt teachings and manner of life. The sect probably took its name from the founder. Some wish to identify him with Nicholas, one of the seven deacons ordained at Jerusalem.[31] St. Paul had warned Timothy of errors similar to those of the

---

[29] Hebrews xiii, 23.

[30] II Timothy I, 7; iv, 2.

Nicolaites: "Some shall depart from the faith, giving heed to spirits of error and doctrines of devils. Speaking lies and hypocrisy and having their conscience seared. Forbidding to marry, to abstain from meats."[32]

Christ does not say that He hates the Nicolaites. He hates only their evil works and their errors. This teaches us that we must ever hate all error, but love the erring, especially those who err through no fault of their own. Our love for them should show itself in earnest efforts to bring them to the knowledge and love of truth.

7. A great reward is promised to those who overcome heresy and sin by reclaiming the wandering to the true Faith. "To him that overcometh I will give to eat of the tree of life." Christ Himself is this tree of life whose fruit is the Holy Eucharist on earth, and eternal union with Him in heaven.

---

[31] Acts of the Apostles vi, 5

[32] I Timothy iv, 1-3; cf. also Irenaeus "Adversus Haereses" xxvi, 3.

TO THE CHURCH OF SMYRNA

CHAPTER II

8. And to the angel of the church of Smyrna write: These things saith the First and the Last who was dead and is alive.

9. I know thy tribulation and thy poverty, but thou art rich: and thou art blasphemed by them that say they are Jews and are not, but are the synagogue of Satan.

10. Fear none of those things which thou shalt suffer. Behold, the devil will cast some of you into prison that you may be tried: and you shall have tribulation ten days. Be thou faithful unto death: and I will give thee the crown of life.

11. He that hath an ear, let him hear what the spirit saith to the churches. He that shall overcome, shall not be hurt by the second death.

8. Smyrna is an important city on the bay of Smyrna, thirty-five miles north of Ephesus. At present it is a mandatory of Greece and numbers 250,000 inhabitants. Christianity was brought to Smyrna at a very early date. The Jews of this city were especially hostile to the Gospel. The "angel" of Smyrna was most probably St. John's own disciple, St. Polycarp.

9. The bishop is praised for his patience in suffering and for his poverty. He is poor indeed in this world's goods, but he is rich in the grace of God and in true Christian Charity. He has suffered much on account of calumnies spread by the Jews of Smyrna.

The real Jew — the true son of Abraham — is the Christian who has accepted Christ as the Messias promised to Abraham of old. These who call themselves Jews are but rebels against the God of Israel and the prophets of old. They are the "synagogue of Satan." Wherever the Gospel was preached the Jews were its first and most bitter enemies. Tertullian writes: "The Jewish synagogues are the source of persecutions."[33]

10. These Jewish enemies of the Gospel will succeed in bringing on a persecution, but it shall be of short duration. The Christians must suffer for

---

[33] Tertullian, "Scorpiace" 10; cf. Romans ii, 28; St. Matthew xxiii, 34.

their Faith, yet there is nothing to fear; he who perseveres will obtain the crown of eternal life. This prophecy found a fulfillment in the persecution which raged for a short time at Smyrna about the year 155 A. D. St. Polycarp was its most illustrious victim. An account of his martyrdom was written by his brethren to notify the neighboring churches of their bishop's death. This work, known as the "Martyrdom of Polycarp," shows that the Jews took an active part in the persecution.[34]

11. Those who suffer for the Faith seem to be overcome by their enemies, but if they persevere unto the end they are the real victors. They suffer death of the body, but thereby win eternal life. "He that shall lose his life for my sake, shall find it."[35] He need not fear the second death which is eternal damnation of body and soul.[36]

---

[34] Eusebius, "Church History" Iv, 15; Martyrdom of Polycarp xiii.

[35] St. Matthew xvi, 25; St. James i, 12.

[36] Apocalypse xx, 14.

TO THE CHURCH OF PERGAMUS

CHAPTER II

12. And to the angel of the church of Pergamus write: These things saith he that hath the sharp two-edged sword:

13. I know where thou dwellest, where the seat of Satan is: and thou holdest fast my name, and hast not denied my faith. Even in those days when Antipas was my faithful witness, who was slain amongst you where Satan dwelleth.

14. But I have against thee a few things: because thou hast there them that hold the doctrine of Balaam, who taught Balac to cast a stumbling-block before the children of Israel, to eat and to commit fornication.

15. So thou hast also them that hold the doctrines of the Nicolaites.

10. In like manner do penance: or else I will come to thee quickly and will fight against thee with the sword of my mouth.

17. He that hath an ear, let him hear what the spirit saith to the churches. To him that overcometh, I will give the hidden manna, and will give him a white counter, and in the counter, a new name written, which no man knoweth, but he that receiveth it.

12. Pergamus, one of the most magnificent cities of ancient times, was located on the River Caicus about fifteen miles from the sea and sixty miles north of Smyrna. It seems that paganism was deeply rooted at Pergamas. Tacitus mentions its famous temple to Aesculapius, the god of medicine.[37] There was also a number of the immoral Nicolaites at Pergamus. Persecution had already broken out there in the time of St. John. At least one Christian had valiantly met death for his Faith. In later times Pergamus gave other martyrs for Christ. Eusebius mentions Carpus, Papylus and Agathonice who were executed in March 250 A. D.[38]

Today the city is known as Bergama and numbers about 20,000 inhabitants, mostly Turks and Greek schismatics. The ruins of three ancient

---

[37] Tacitus "Annales" iii, 63.

[38] Eusebius, "Church History" IV, xv, 48.

churches were discovered in 1878-86. One of them had been a magnificent basilica dedicated to St. John.

Gaius, to whom St. John addressed his third Epistle, is said to have been the first bishop of Pergamus.[39] If this be true, he was most probably the "angel" to whom St. John now writes.

13. Pergamus is called "Satan's Throne," on account of its deep-rooted paganism, its persecution of the Christians, and the immoralities of the Nicolaites. There may also be a reference to worship offered to the statue of the emperor. It seems that Pergamus was still the capital of proconsular Asia at that time. If so, it had a statue of the emperor to which sacrifice must be offered under pain of death. This would account for the persecution in which Antipas suffered martyrdom.[40]

14, 15. The bishop of Pergamus is praised for his zeal and constancy in the face of persecution. Yet there is some room for complaint. He has not been sufficiently energetic in rooting out the hated Nicolaite heresy. Some of his flock are holding this evil doctrine. On account of their immoral teachings and practices they are called disciples of Balaam. This is a reference to the Moabites who went among the Israelites at Balaam's suggestion to seduce them into idolatry and adultery.[41] In like manner the Nicolaites are seducing the faithful into sin and error.

16. Unless those wicked ones do penance they shall be smitten with the two-edged sword which breaks the obstinate and confounds all sin and error. There may also be a reference here to the fate of the Moabites who had seduced the children of Israel.[42]

17. He who overcomes sin and error shall receive the hidden manna of eternal joy through union with Christ in heaven — a union that begins on earth in the worthy reception of the Holy Eucharist. The same reward was promised to the bishop of Ephesus under the symbol of the tree of life.[43]

The eternal joys of heaven are also symbolized by a white pebble ("counter" in the Douay version) upon which a new name is written. It were useless to speculate on this name since Christ says "no man knoweth but he that receiveth it." It is probably the "new name" mentioned below in

---

[39] Apostolic Constitutions vii, 46.

[40] Cf. below, on xiii, 17.

[41] Numbers xxxi, 16.

[42] Numbers xxxi, 17.

[43] See above.

chapter xix, 12. Why the joys of heaven should be symbolized by a white pebble is not known. Gigot says there is probably a reference to some use of a "white stone" familiar to St. John's readers, but unknown to us.[44]

---

[44] "The Apocalypse of St. John," Westminster version, page 6.

TO THE CHURCH OF THYATIRA

CHAPTER II

18. And to the angel of the church of Thyatira write: These things saith the Son of God, who hath his eyes like to a flame of fire, and his feet like fine brass.

19. I know thy works, and thy faith, and thy charity, and thy ministry, and thy patience, and thy last works which are more than the former.

20. But I have against thee a few things: because thou sufferest the woman Jezabel, who calleth herself a prophetess, to teach and to seduce my servants, to commit fornication, and to eat things sacrificed to idols.

21. And I gave her a time that she might do penance, and she will not repeat of her fornication.

22. Behold, I will cast her into a bed: and they that commit adultery with her shall be in great tribulation, except they do penance from their deeds.

23. And I will kill her children with death, and all the churches shall know that I am he that searcheth the reins and hearts, and I will give to every one of you according to your works. But to you I say:

24. And to the rest who are at Thyatira: Whosoever have not this doctrine, and who have not known the depths of Satan, as they say, I will not put upon you any other burden.

25. Yet that which you have, hold fast till I come.

26. And he that shall overcome and keep my words unto the end, I will give him power over the nations.

27. And he shall rule them with a rod of iron, and as the vessel of a potter they shall be broken,

28. As I also have received of my Father: and I will give him the morning star.

29. He that hath an ear, let him hear what the spirit saith to the churches.

18. Fifty miles southeast of Pergamus lay the ancient city of Thyatira. Diana was greatly venerated here as at Ephesus, but Apollo was the chief divinity in whose honor games were celebrated. Lydia, a woman converted

by St. Paul at Philippi, was from Thyatira.[45] At the beginning of the third century the population was almost entirely Christian.[46]

In the Middle Ages the Turks changed the name of Thyatira to Ak-Hissar (White Fortress). The population today numbers about 22,000, mostly Mahomedans and Greek schismatics.

19, 20. The bishop of Thyatira is praised for his faith and for his good work in the ministry. Unlike Timothy, his zeal has increased, yet there is one fault for which he is reproved. He has not sufficiently guarded the faithful against the teachings of a certain false prophetess who is stigmatized as "a Jezabel." Through the influence of Jezabel, King Achab fell into idolatry and became the most wicked of Israel's rulers.[47] In like manner the Christians of Thyatira were being led into the doctrines of the Nicolaites by a wicked woman who called herself a prophetess. She was even seducing them to partake of the sacrificial banquets of the pagans.[48]

21, 22. St. John compares heresy to adultery. This figure of speech is often found in the Old Testament. Christ is the true and only spouse of souls. Heresy is an act of unfaithfulness to Him.

Our Lord has shown special mercy by giving this false prophetess and her followers time to repent, but they will not repent of their sins. They are now threatened with severe punishments. They shall be stricken down with sickness and death. All the churches must realize that Christ will tolerate neither heresy nor schism.

24, 25. The faithful of Thyatira are admonished to avoid the doctrines of heretics, and to guard carefully the Faith that has been preached to them. No other commandment is needed for them.

The Nicolaites were followers of the Gnostics who boasted of a higher knowledge of divine things possessed by them alone. They called it the "abyss" or "depth" of knowledge. St. John shows the true nature of this so-called knowledge when he names it the "depths of Satan."

26, 27. The faithful are warned of the necessity of good works for salvation. Those who persevere in them unto the end shall have part with Christ in the judgment of the wicked. They shall participate in the power He has received from the Father — power to rule the nations with a rod of

---

[45] Acts of the Apostles xvi, 13, 14.

[46] St. Epiphanius, "Contra Haereses" 11, 33.

[47] III Kings xvi, 31-34; xxi, 25.

[48] Cf. I Corinthians viii.

iron.[49] St. Paul teaches the same truth: "Know ye not that the saints shall judge this world?"[50]

28. To those who persevere, our Lord will give the eternal glory of the Beatific Vision in heaven. Christ, the Morning Star, shall be the object of this vision because He is God, equal in all things to the Father. This same reward was promised to the other churches under slightly different symbols.[51]

Christ is referred to as a star in the prophecy of Balaam: "A star shall arise out of Jacob."[52] In another passage of the Apocalypse Christ calls Himself the "bright and morning Star."[53] By the reflected light of this Star "the just shall shine as the sun in the kingdom of their Father."[54]

---

[49] Cf. Psalm ii, 9.

[50] I Corinthians vi, 2.

[51] Cf. vv. 7, 10, 17.

[52] Numbers xxiv, 17.

[53] Apocalypse xxii, 16.

[54] St. Matthew xiii, 43.

TO THE CHURCH OF SARDIS

CHAPTER III

1. And to the angel of the church of Sardis write: These things saith he that hath the seven spirits of God, and the seven stars: I know thy works, that thou hast the name of being alive: and thou art dead.

2. Be watchful and strengthen the things that remain, which are ready to die. For I find not thy works full before my God.

3. Have in mind therefore in what manner thou hast received and heard: and observe, and do penance. If then thou shalt not watch: I will come to thee as a thief, and thou shalt not know at what hour I will come to thee.

4. But thou hast a few names in Sardis, which have not defiled their garments: and they shall walk with me in white, because they are worthy.

5. He that shall overcome shall thus be clothed in white garments, and I will not blot out his name out of the book of life, and I will confess his name before my Father, and before the angels.

6. He that hath an ear, let him hear what the spirit saith to the churches.

1. Sardis, the capital of Lydia, was a city of considerable importance. It was about thirty miles south of Thyatira on the Pactolus, which flowed through its market-place. It was noted for its commercial activities and for the manufacture of carpets and woolen goods. It was also the residence of the famous Croesus. The straggling village of Sart now marks the site of this ancient city.

"He who has the seven spirits" is the sovereign Lord of the seven spirits who stand before the throne of God. Some interpreters take these words to mean that Christ possesses the fulness of the gifts of the Holy Ghost. "And the spirit of the Lord shall rest upon him: the spirit of wisdom and of understanding, the spirit of counsel and fortitude the spirit of knowledge and of godliness. And he shall be filled with the spirit of the fear of the Lord."[55]

He who has the seven stars is Christ who exercises a special care for the ministers of His Church. He is now manifesting this solicitude for the

---

[55] Isaias xi, 2, 3.

bishop of Sardis. Christ, the searcher of hearts and reins, knows the true state of this bishop's soul. He appears to be a faithful servant of God and a true shepherd of souls, but in reality he is spiritually dead. These words imply a state of moral sin and a sad neglect of pastoral duty.

2-5. Through the ministry of St. John, Christ now exhorts the bishop of Sardis to arouse himself to a realization of his sad plight. He must do penance for the past and stir up his zeal to save the few members of his flock who remain faithful.

The pastor of souls is responsible to God for their salvation. He must teach and guide them by word and example, "for the lips of the priest shall keep knowledge, and they shall seek the law at his mouth, because he is the angel of the Lord of hosts."[56] He is like a watchman set upon a watch-tower; "if he see the sword coming, and sound not the trumpet and the people look not to themselves, and the sword come, and cut off a soul from among them; he indeed is taken away in his iniquity, but I will require his blood at the hand of the watchman."[57]

These words of the prophet are also a warning that no one can make an unworthy pastor an excuse for his sins. He still has the teachings of the Church and the grace of the Sacraments which are always efficacious whether administered by a worthy or an unworthy pastor. Even when the watchman does not give warning the soul that perishes "is taken away in his iniquity."

The pastor who is negligent in the care of his people is exposed to the danger of being snatched away by sudden death without the grace of the Sacraments. Unfortunately, the church of Sardis is in very sad condition, yet it numbers a few faithful souls who shall be saved. They shall be clothed with the white garments of eternal happiness.

---

[56] Malachias ii, 7.

[57] Isaias xxxiii, 6.

TO THE CHURCH OF PHILADELPHIA

CHAPTER III

7. And to the angel of the church of Philadelphia write: These things saith the Holy One and the true one, he that hath the key of David; he that openeth and no man shutteth: shutteth and no man openeth.

8. I know thy works. Behold, I have given before thee a door opened which no man can shut: because thou hast little strength and hast kept my word and hast not denied my name.

9. Behold I will bring of the synagogue of Satan, who say they are Jews, and are not, but do lie. Behold. I will make them come and adore before thy feet. And they shall know that I have loved thee.

10. Because thou hast kept the word of my patience, I will also keep thee from the hour of temptation, which shall come upon the whole world to try them that dwell upon earth.

11. Behold I come quickly: hold fast that which thou hast, that no man take thy crown.

12. He that shall overcome, I will make him a pillar in the temple of my God: and he shall go out no more: and I will write upon him the name of my God, and the name of the city of my God, the new Jerusalem which Cometh down out of heaven from my God, and my new name.

13. He that hath an ear, let him hear what the spirit saith to the churches.

7. By following the valley of the Cogamus south-eastward from Sardis for about thirty miles St. John's messenger would come to Philadelphia. The city was founded by Philadelphus, king of Pergamon, but became a Roman possession in 133 B. C. It was practically destroyed by an earthquake in 17 A. D. On account of the assistance then given by Tiberius the name was changed to Neocaesarea. The modern city, known as Ala-Shehr, is a station on the Smyrna-Dinair railway and has a population of about 20,000.

According to the Constitutions of the Apostles, Demetrius was the first bishop of Philadelphia.[58] He must have been appointed by St. John and is probably the "angel" here addressed. The apologist Miltiades mentions a prophetess Ammia who must have belonged to the primitive church of Philadelphia.[59]

As true God, Christ calls Himself the True and Holy One. He holds the key of David since He possesses the eternal kingdom promised to David;[60] "The Lord God shall give unto him the throne of David his father; and he shall reign in the house of Jacob forever. And of his kingdom there shall be no end."[61] In this kingdom our Lord reigns supreme. There is none to challenge His authority; He opens and no man closes; He closes and no man opens.

8-10. The bishop of Philadelphia has but few of those natural qualifications which human wisdom deems necessary for the high office entrusted to him. Yet he has been faithful to his trust: he has kept Christ's commandment of patient perseverance. Christ now promises him protection in time of persecution and temptation. He shall even have the grace to make converts from among the obstinate Jews, — from that "synagogue of Satan."

Not to the great and learned, but to the humble and faithful does God promise His graces. "The weak things of this world hath God chosen that He may confound the strong."[62] In choosing the weak to overcome the strong our Lord plainly teaches that He is supreme pastor in His Church. He needs not human power nor human wisdom. For this reason did He choose twelve poor ignorant men as Apostles to carry the Gospel to all nations.

Through this faithful bishop our Lord promises special grace and protection to all faithful pastors at the time of Antichrist — "that hour of temptation which shall come upon the whole world to try them that dwell upon earth." This is the first intimation that apostasy from the Faith will not be general in the days of Antichrist. There will always be souls faithful to Christ with faithful shepherds to guide them.

11. Grace is always promised on condition of perseverance: "Guard well what thou hast, lest another receive the crown destined for thee."

[58] Constitutions of the Apostles vii, 45.

[59] Eusebius, "Church History V, xvii.

[60] II Kings vii, 16.

[61] St. Luke i, 32, 33.

[62] I Corinthians i, 27.

12. All faithful bishops are apostles and pillars of the Church here on earth.[63] They shall also be blessed and honored citizens of the Church triumphant, — the new-Jerusalem.

---

[63] Cf. Galatians ii, 9.

TO THE CHURCH OF LAODICEA

CHAPTER III

14. And to the angel of the church of Laodicea write: These things saith the Amen, the faithful and true witness, who is the beginning of the creation of God:

15. I know thy works that thou art neither cold nor hot. I would that thou wert cold or hot.

16. But because thou art lukewarm, and neither cold nor hot, I will begin to vomit thee out of my mouth.

17. Because thou sayest: I am rich, and made wealthy, and have need of nothing; and knowest not that thou art wretched, and miserable, and poor, and blind, and naked.

18. I counsel thee to buy of me gold fire-tried, that thou mayest be made rich: and mayest be clothed in white garments, and that the shame of thy nakedness may not appear: and anoint thy eyes with eye-salve, that thou mayest see.

19. Such as I love I rebuke and chastize. Be zealous therefore and do penance.

20. Behold, I stand at the gate and knock. If any man shall hear my voice and open to me the door, I will come in to him, and will sup with him, and he with me.

21. To him that shall overcome, I will give to sit with me in my throne: as I also have overcome, and am set down with my Father in his throne.

22. He that hath an ear, let him hear what the spirit saith to the churches.

14. Laodicea was an important city of Phrygia about 50 miles southeast of Philadelphia on the river Lycus. Antiochus II colonized it about 250 B. C. and gave it the name of his wife, Laodice. Laodicea was a center of industries and commerce and especially famous for its woolen goods and sandals. It was also the seat of a medical school.

The Gospel had been preached in Laodicea by St. Paul's disciple Epaphras. The house of Nymphas was used as a place of worship for the little Christian community.[64] The Constitutions of the Apostles mentions

St. Nymphas as the first bishop of Laodicea.[65] St. Paul wrote a letter to the Christians of Laodicea which has been lost.[66]

Jesus Christ is the Amen, — the unchangeable and eternal. By Him were all things created: "Thou in the beginning, Lord, didst found the earth. And the works of thy hands are the heavens."[67]

15-17. The bishop of Laodicea is lukewarm and indifferent. Hence our Lord is about to reject him. He withdraws the graces that have been neglected. Christ would prefer to find the bishop entirely cold, because there would be more hopes for him. He would more easily realize his condition and do penance. Tepid souls easily deceive themselves, believing they are rich in God's grace when in reality they are in a miserable state, stripped of God's grace and blinded to their true condition.

The reference to riches may also imply that the bishop of Laodicea had given himself too much to the acquisition of worldly goods. He thus became the very opposite of St. Polycarp who was poor in material goods, but rich in the grace and love of God.

18. The bishop is commanded to arouse himself from this spiritual lethargy. Instead of the base gold of earthly riches, he must obtain the pure gold of charity and zeal, — a gold purified in the fire of trials and temptations. Thus shall he clothe himself with the white garments of grace. Then will his eyes be opened to a proper knowledge of the things of God.

19, 20. Trials and afflictions are proof of God's mercy and love. They arouse the soul to greater fervor. Christ is ever patient and loving. He stands at the door of our soul ready to bestow His graces and blessings. But the soul must cooperate; it must open the door to Him.

21. A share in the glories of Christ in heaven is promised to those who cooperate with His graces and persevere unto the end.

These warnings to the churches show Christ's solicitude for our salvation. They also prove His deep concern for those charged with the care of souls.

---

[64] Colossians iv, 13-15.

[65] Constitutions of the Apostles vii, 46.

[66] Colossians iv, 16.

[67] Hebrews i, 10.

THE CONSTITUTION OF THE CHURCH

CHAPTER IV

1. After these things, I looked and behold, a door was opened in heaven, and the first voice which I heard, as it were the voice of a trumpet speaking with me, said: Come np hither, and I will shew thee the things which must be done hereafter.

2. And immediately I was in the spirit: and behold there was a throne set in heaven, and upon the throne one sitting.

3. And he that sat was to the sight like jasper and the sardine stone: and there was a rainbow about the throne, in sight like unto an emerald.

4. And round about the throne were four and twenty seats: and upon the seats, four and twenty ancients sitting, clothed in white garments, and on their heads were crowns of gold.

1. Chapters iv-v serve as an introduction to the visions which follow. They describe the constitution of the church on earth, and the worship which it gives to Jesus Christ the Lamb of God.

The prophet sees the throne of God surrounded by the Apostles, the Evangelists, the faithful, and angels with censers of sweet-smelling incense. Beneath the throne are the martyrs who have suffered for their Faith, and in front of it stand the seven burning lamps. In the midst of the throne stands the Lamb of God as if slain.

He is worthy of all honor and praise. All bow down in adoration to Him who alone is able to break the seals of the future.

This vision of adoration is a symbol of the worship offered to God in His Church on earth. The throne of God is the altar upon which the Lamb is mystically slain in the holy sacrifice of the Mass. Before Him all the faithful bow down in adoration and sing their canticles of praise. In ancient times the bishop had his throne behind the altar, and round about it on either side sat the priests and other clergy. During solemn Mass lighted lamps stood around the altar and ministers carried vessels of burning incense. Beneath the altar reposed the relics of martyrs who had suffered for their faith.

2. The door opened in heaven is a figure of speech signifying that St. John was wrapped in ecstasy even as St. Paul had been many years before.[68] While in this ecstasy he sees the future of the Church unfolded before him in symbolic visions such as were seen by the[69] prophets of old.

3. The red and orange colors of the jasper and sardonyx signify the infinite justice of God. The rainbow of emerald is a symbol of God's mercy and love which save man by calling him to penance. In the days of Noe the bow was set in the heavens as a sign of mercy and forgiveness. Thus at the very beginning of these prophecies God reveals Himself as a just Judge and a kind Father.

4. The four and twenty ancients are the twelve patriarchs of the Old Law and the twelve Apostles of the New Dispensation. By extension they represent the bishops and priests of the Church throughout the centuries. They are seated upon thrones participating with Christ in the government of His Church. They wear the crowns of royalty because they have been chosen kings and princes in the kingdom of God on earth.[70] The gold is a symbol of Christian charity. The white garments signify sanctifying grace and the eternal happiness to which it leads.

CHAPTER IV

5. And from the throne proceeded lightnings, and voices and thunders: and there were seven lamps burning before the throne, which are the seven spirits of God.

6. And in the sight of the throne was as it were a sea of glass like to crystal: and in the midst of the throne and round about the throne were four living creatures full of eyes before and behind.

7. And the first living creature was like a lion: and the second living creature like a calf; and the third living creature having the face, as it were, of a man: and the fourth living creature was like an eagle flying.

8. And the four living creatures had each of them six wings; and round about and within they are full of eyes. And they rested not day and night, saying: Holy, Holy, Holy, Lord God Almighty, who was, and who is, and who is to come.

---

[68] II Corinthians xii, 2.

[69] Genesis ix, 12-17.

[70] Apocalypse i, 6.

9. And when those living creatures gave glory and honor and benediction to him that sitteth on the throne, who liveth for ever and ever, 10, the four and twenty ancients fell down before him that sitteth on the throne, and adored him that liveth for ever and ever, and cast their crowns before the throne saying:

11. Thou art worthy. O Lord our God, to receive glory and honor, and power: because thou hast created all things, and for thy will they were, and have been created.

5. As of old on mount Sinai, thunder and lightning are symbols of God's power and majesty.[71] On the last day our Lord shall come on the clouds of heaven as the "lightning cometh out of the east and appeareth even into the west."[72]

The voice is the voice of the Church preaching the Gospel to all nations. The thunders are the warnings of the Gospel against the wicked who refuse to accept its teachings. The seven lamps are the seven angels who stand before the throne of God, and by extension, all angels. They are the instructors and enlighteners of men. For this reason they are compared to lighted lamps. The ministery of angels in the Church is apparent on every page of the Apocalypse. They also represent bishop and pastors in the Church.[73]

6. In Biblical symbolism the sea represents human society.[74] Here the sea of crystal is the Church, — the society of the faithful permeated by the light of divine truth which Christ brought to earth.

The four living creatures are the four greater prophets of the Old Law and the four Evangelists of the New Law. The number "four" signifies the universality of the Church which carries the Gospel to the four quarters of the earth. The eyes before and behind and round about the living creatures also refer to the universality of the Church in time and place. They see on all sides and have regard to all times, both before and after Christ, from the creation of the world until its final consummation.

---

[71] Exodus xix, 16-8.

[72] St. Matthew xxiv, 27; xxvi, 64.

[73] See above.

[74] Cf. Daniel vii, .2,3; Isaias lvii, 20; lx, 3 sq.; St. Matthew xiii, 47; Apocalypse xvii, 15.

7. The four creatures symbolize the principal virtues necessary for those who preach the Gospel of Christ. The lion is a symbol of strength and courage; the ox, of patient labor. The creature with the face of a man denotes reason and prudence. The eagle in flight represents contemplation. From the earliest times the Evangelists have been represented in art by these four living creatures.

8. Each of the four living creatures has six wings. In this they resemble the seraphim in the vision of Isaias. The symbolism is probably the same. With two wings the seraphim shielded themselves before the majesty of God. These were adoration and reverential awe. With the wings of humility and temperance they veiled their feet. The two wings which served for flight symbolize faith and prayer.[75]

9, 10. All creatures must ever proclaim the power and majesty of God who is thrice holy in the ever blessed Trinity. But no creature is worthy to wear a crown in the presence of God. The four and twenty ancients lay their crowns at the foot of the throne to acknowledge that God alone is head of the Church. It is only in dependence upon Him that they govern.

11. All power, honor, and glory belong to Him who created all things. What sublime theology the Apocalypse contains! Its every word teaches some exalted truth concerning God, or recalls to mind some noble Christian duty!

CHAPTER V

1. And I saw in the right hand of him that sat on the throne, a book written within and without, sealed with seven seals.

2. And I saw a strong angel, proclaiming with a loud voice: Who is worthy to open the book, and to loose the seals thereof?

3. And no man was able, neither in heaven, nor on earth nor under the earth, to open the book, nor to look on it.

4. And I wept much, because no man was found worthy to open nor to see it.

5. And one of the ancients said to me: Weep not; for behold the lion of the tribe of Juda, the root of David hath prevailed to open the book, and to loose the seven seals thereof.

6. And I saw, and behold in the midst of the throne and of the four living creatures, and in the midst of the ancients, a Lamb standing as it were

---

[75] Isaias vi, 2, 3.

slain, having seven horns and seven eyes: which are the seven spirits of God sent forth into all the earth.

The preceding chapter is devoted to the Church and the worship it offers to Almighty God. It depicts the faithful paying homage of adoration, praise and thanksgiving through the ministry of Apostles, bishops and priests. The present chapter is taken up with our divine Savior, the head and spouse of His Church. He alone is able to open the book of its future. He is also worthy of divine honors in the Blessed Sacrament of the altar no less than in heaven.

1. In the right hand of God, St. John sees the book of the Church's future history; but the book is sealed to all creatures. No one in heaven nor on earth, nor under the earth knows what the future holds in store unless God deigns to reveal it.

In ancient times a book consisted of a long strip of parchment or papyrus wound around a stick to which it was fastened. It thus resembled the roll of a player-piano. The writing was on the side of the parchment that rolled in. The roll which St. John saw in the vision was written on both sides and sealed down with seven seals. The writing on both sides symbolizes fulness of knowledge concerning the future. The number "seven" also indicates completeness or universality as noted above.[76] Consequently the Apocalypse embraces the entire history of the Church from the time of Christ until the consummation of the world.

3-6. Christ, — the lion of the tribe of Juda, — is alone found worthy to break the seven seals and open the book. In this vision St. John sees our Lord in His sacred humanity. It is the same Christ whom the Baptist pointed out as the Lamb of God. His standing attitude becomes the triumphant Savior. He is upon the throne of God because of His divinity. He is true God of true God, equal in all things to the Father.

The appearance of being slain is a reference to the holy sacrifice of the Mass in which Christ is mystically sacrificed although He stands triumphant at the right hand of the Father in heaven.

The seven horns and seven eyes are the seven spirits of God, — the angels whom Christ sends forth into the world as His ministers. Angels also represent the bishops and priests whom our Lord sends to teach and

---

[76] See above.

govern His faithful.[77] The seven spirits may also signify the graces and gifts of the Holy Ghost showered upon the Church.[78]

Horns are symbols of power. Thus Zachary calls our Lord "a horn of salvation."[79] The eyes signify the omniscience of Christ; all times and all things are present to His view.

CHAPTER V

7. And he came and took the book out of the right hand of him that sat on the throne.

8. And when he had opened the book, the four living creatures, and the four and twenty ancients fell down before the Lamb, having every one of them harps, and golden vials full of odors, which are the prayers of the saints.

9. And they sang a new canticle, saying: Thou art worthy, O Lord, to take the book, and to open the seals thereof: because thou wast slain, and hast redeemed us to God, in thy blood, out of every tribe, and tongue, and people, and nation.

10. And hast made us to our God a kingdom and priests, and we shall reign on earth.

11. And I beheld and I heard the voice of many angels around about the throne, and the living creatures and the ancients: and the number of them was thousands of thousands, 12, saying with a loud voice: The Lamb that was slain is worthy to receive power, and divinity, and wisdom, and strength, and honor, and glory, and benediction.

13. And every creature which is in heaven, and on earth, and under the earth, and such as are in the seas, and all that are in them: I heard all saying: To him that sitteth on the throne, and to the Lamb, benediction, and honor, and glory, and power for ever and ever.

14. And the four living creatures said: Amen. And the four and twenty ancients fell down on their faces: and adored him that liveth for ever and ever.

7. The Lamb receives the book of the future from the hand of God. Knowledge of the future does not belong to the human nature of Christ; it

---

[77] See above.

[78] See above.

[79] St. Luke i, 69.

is imparted to His human intellect by the hypostatic union of the human and divine natures in the one divine person.

8. When the book is opened all ministers of the Church bow down in adoration before God and the Lamb. As priests they offer to Christ the praises of His Church. They also present to Him golden vials and sweet perfumes, — symbols of the prayers and good works of all the faithful.

9. The whole Church of Christ now sends up a new canticle of praise. It is the canticle of the New Law in honor of our divine Savior. His faithful followers never weary of proclaiming His divinity and the glory He has given to God by the redemption of the world.

10. It is for the glory of God that Christ has chosen some to be ministers of His Church, and to rule it upon earth. He has also made them priests to lay before the throne of God the prayers and praises of all His people. The faithful have some fellowship in these great privileges. They can unite with the priests of the Church in offering sacrifices of praise and thanksgiving to God. Hence St. Peter says: "You are a chosen generation, a kingly priesthood, a holy nation."[80]

11-14. "Thousands of angels join the glad acclaim. Their song arouses the whole universe. From the heights of the firmament, from the sea and its lowest depths, from the breast of every creature . . . rise the voices which embrace their supreme God and His Christ in one common act of adoration: Blessing, honor, glory, and power be unto Him that is seated on the throne, and to the Lamb for ever."[81]

---

[80] I Peter ii, 9.

[81] Fouard, "St. John," page 100 (Eng. Translation).

PERSECUTIONS OF THE CHURCH AND FALL OF THE PAGAN EMPIRE AT ROME

CHAPTER VI

1. And I saw the Lamb had opened one of the seven seals, and I heard one of the four living creatures, as it were the voice of thunder, saying: Come and see.

2. And I saw; and behold a white horse, and he that sat on him had a bow, and there was a crown given him, and he went forth conquering that he might conquer.

3. And when he had opened the second seal, I heard the second living creature, saying: Come and see.

4. And there went out another horse that was red: and to him that sat thereon, it was given that he should take peace from the earth, and that they should kill one another, and a great sword was given to him.

5. And when he had opened the third seal, I heard the third living creature saying: Come and see. And behold a black horse, and he that sat on him had a pair of scales in his hand.

6. And I heard as it were a voice in the midst of the four living creatures, saying: Two pounds of wheat for a penny, and thrice two pounds of barley for a penny, and see that thou hurt not the wine and the oil.

With this chapter begin those symbolic visions in which the entire history of the Church is unfolded before us. The first part (chapters vi-viii) extends from the which the entire history of the Church is unfolded before Christ. Some of the prophecies in this part have been fulfilled, as a comparison with the events of the past nineteen centuries will show. As noted in the introduction,[82] application of these prophecies to history must be confined to generalities because the Apostle is not giving detailed accounts. In many cases the same prophecy may refer to several events of similar nature. Hence a prophecy may have been fulfilled in the past and still refer to similar events in the future.

---

[82] See above.

Toward the end of this chapter there is a glimpse of the last days of the world. This is to show that the whole history of the Church has an intimate connection with the second coming of Jesus Christ. In fact the mission of the Church throughout the ages is to prepare mankind for that great event.

1. The voice of thunder is the voice of the Church resounding to the uttermost parts of the earth as it proclaims the Gospel to all nations and threatens the wicked with trials and punishments.

2. White horses were used by Roman conquerors when celebrating triumphs for their victories. The rider with the bow symbolizes the pagan empire of Rome waging war against the Church. The white horse and the crown of a triumphing general signify that the empire will appear victorious for a time in its conflict with the new-born Church.

This verse clearly foretells the terrible persecutions launched against the Church with all the powers of the Roman empire, then undisputed mistress of the world. These persecutions continued almost without interruption from the time of Nero in 64 A. D. until the victory of Constantine in 312 A. D. But it was not until Theodosius in 394 A. D. that Christianity completely triumphed over paganism.

3, 4. The red horse signifies war as the context clearly indicates. This is a prediction of the many wars and internal troubles that harassed the Roman empire before its final overthrow by the barbarian hordes from the North.

5, 6. In the wake of war follow pestilence and famine foreshadowed by the black horse. The sixth verse explicitly predicts times of famine when the necessities of life sell for exorbitant prices. The English version does not bring out this idea clearly. In Greek it is a dry measure equal to one and one-half pints. Our bushel contains 42 of these Greek measures. A "penny" is the translation of the Greek word σεντ a Roman coin worth about 17 cents in our money. It was an ordinary day's wage for a workingman.[83] At this rate it would require 21 days' labor for a bushel of wheat, and 7 days for a bushel of barley.

The chastisements of God are always tempered with mercy. They are not to destroy man, but to convert him. Hence not all foods shall fail during these famines. This is indicated by the command to leave the wine and oil unharmed.

CHAPTER VI

---

[83] Cf. St. Matthew xx, 2.

7. And when he had opened the fourth seal, I heard the voice of the four living creatures, saying: Come and see.

8. And behold a pale horse, and he that sat upon him, his name was death, and hell followed him. And power was given him over the four parts of the earth, to kill with sword, with famine, and with death, and with the beasts of the earth.

9. And when he had opened the fifth seal, I saw under the altar the souls of them that were slain for the word of God, and for the testimony which they held.

10. And they cried out with a loud voice, saying: How long, O Lord, holy and true, dost thou not judge and revenge our blood on them that dwell on earth?

11. And white robes were given to every one of them one. And it was said to them, that they should rest for a little time, till their fellow servants and their brethren, who were to be slain, even as they, should be filled up.

8. Death riding upon the pale horse is followed by hell. If this be the hell of the damned, the prophecy must refer to the death of the wicked, especially the persecutors. It is worthy of note that nearly all the Emperors who persecuted the Church were taken off by tragic or violent death. It is more probable, however, that "hell" here corresponds to the Hebrew "sheol," a general term for the abode of the dead.

Death is given power to destroy by every sort of plague, the chief of which are war, famine, and pestilence. Such were the chastisements inflicted upon the pagan Empire of Rome for persecuting the Church. Such will be the punishment of every nation that follows in her footsteps. We have seen this prophecy fulfilled in our own day upon nations that sought to oppress and destroy the Church of Christ.

9, 10. At the breaking of the fifth seal St. John sees the souls of the martyrs beneath the altar where they enjoy eternal happiness in union with Christ, yet they cry out for justice. They beseech God to manifest His glory, His justice, and His mercy by the resurrection of their bodies, the punishment of His enemies and the general judgment of all men.

The imagery of this vision seems to refer to the altar of holocaust which stood in the inner court of the temple before the Holy Place. In the Jewish ritual the blood of the victim was poured out at the foot of the altar.[84]

---

[84] Leviticus iv, 7.

The life of the victim was said to be in the blood: "The life of the flesh is in the blood," and again, "Beware of this that thou eat not the blood, for the blood is for the soul, and therefore thou must not eat the soul with the flesh."[85] Hence the life or soul of the victim was conceived as being under the altar. In like manner the souls of the martyrs are seen beneath the altar because they too have become victims to God through martyrdom[86] and the voice of their blood cries out to God for justice. "The voice of thy brother's blood crieth out to me from the earth."[87]

11. The martyrs have received the white robes of eternal happiness and glory, but they must wait for the resurrection of the body until the number of their fellow martyrs has been filled up. They have but a short while to wait since the whole course of ages is as a few moments when compared with eternity that follows: "For a thousand years in thy sight are as yesterday which is past, and as a watch in the night."[88]

This verse clearly foretells that there shall be martyrs other than those of the first ages of the Church. There shall be witnesses to God by their blood in every age, especially in the days of Antichrist and at the end of the world. The resurrection and general judgment shall not take place until after this last persecution.

CHAPTER VI

12. And I saw, when he had opened the sixth seal, and behold there was a great earthquake, and the sun became black as sackcloth of hair; and the whole moon became as blood:

13. And the stars fell from heaven upon the earth, as the fig tree casteth its green figs when it is shaken by a great wind.

14. And the heavens departed as a book folded up: and every mountain, and the islands were moved out of their places.

15. And the kings of earth, and the princes, and tribunes, and the rich, and the strong, and every bondman, and every freeman hid themselves in the dens and in the rocks of mountains.

---

[85] Leviticus xvii, 11; Deuteronomy xii, 23.

[86] II Timothy iv, 6; Philippians 11, 17.

[87] Genesis iv, 10.

[88] Psalm lxxxlx, 4.

16. And they said to the mountains and to the rocks: Fall upon us and hide us from the face of him that sitteth upon the throne and from the wrath of the Lamb.

17. For the great day of their wrath is come, and who shall be able to stand?

On the opening of the sixth seal we catch a glimpse of the last persecution and the destruction of the world. This is to show that the prayers of the martyrs have already been heard in the designs of God, and shall be answered in due time.

FALL OF ROMAN EMPIRE

Verses 12-17 have, as we believe, a threefold application:

1° To the fall of the pagan Empire of Rome.

2° To the time of Antichrist.

3° To the end of the world.

In the first two applications the words of the prophecy must bear a symbolic meaning. They were thus interpreted by the early Christians. In the acts of the martyrs the persecution under Diocletian and the internal troubles of the Empire which followed were compared to an earthquake, — an evident allusion to this passage of the Apocalypse.[89]

12. Hence the earthquakes may be interpreted as the great disturbances in society that preceded the fall of the Roman Empire. Like disorders shall foreshadow the coming of Antichrist. The darkening of the sun is a symbol of the weakening of Catholic Faith by the spread of the Arian heresy. A similar weakening of Faith will occur before the days of Antichrist.

The blood color of the moon caused by the darkening of the sun is an omen of wars and persecutions which follow these internal troubles of the Church. This prophecy was fulfilled at the time of the Arian heresy, and during the so-called Reformation of the sixteenth century. Similar wars will attend the coming of Antichrist.

13. In various passages of Scripture stars represent the faithful.[90] In the first chapter of the Apocalypse the bishops of the Church are symbolized by stars.[91] The falling stars predict the defection of large numbers of bishops, priests, and faithful from the true Faith. History shows how these words were verified in the Arian heresy, the Greek schism, and the so-called Reformation.

The stars fall thick and fast like winter figs from a tree shaken by a strong wind. Discord and laxity in church discipline prepare the way for great defections in time of trial and persecution.

---

[89] Cf. also Jeremias 1,46.

[90] Cf. Genesis xxxvii, 9; Daniel viii, 10.

[91] Apocalypse i, 20.

14, 15. The heavens are folded up as a scroll; earthly powers (mountains and islands) are in turmoil. Kings and princes flee for safety. This is a fitting description of the fall of the Roman Empire under the barbarian inroads. The prophecy was also fulfilled in the overthrow of the Byzantine Empire by the Moslems, — a punishment of God for heresy and schism. The prophets of old foretold the fall of ancient empires in similar language.[92]

When applied to the last days of the world these verses bear a more literal interpretation. Then shall "the sun be darkened and the moon shall not give her light, and the stars shall fall from heaven, and the powers of heaven shall be moved."[93] The sun will probably be obscured by volcanic ashes sent up from many places as the result of terrible earthquakes and eruptions of volcanoes. The veiled light of the moon will appear red as blood. Myriads of meteors resembling stars will fall to earth, kindling the whole world into flames. The heavens shall be rolled up as the scroll of a book. In other words, the atmosphere will be so obscured that the sun and moon will become invisible as at the beginning of creation. The mountains and continents shall be overturned and the whole world shall return to chaos.[94]

Comparing this description with the first chapter of Genesis we find the confusion of elements occurring in inverse order to that of their unfolding at creation. The faithful who witness these terrible convulsions of nature will prepare for the judgment of God. They shall be more terrified at the anger of God and of His Christ than by the upheaval of the material world.

16, 17. "Then shall men wither away from fear and expectation of what shall come upon the whole world."[95] They will cry out in their terror: "O ye mountains, fall upon us! Ye hills, cover us!" for "who shall be able to withstand the wrath of God?"[96] This thought is beautifully expressed in the sequence of Masses for the dead:

"Day of wrath, O day of mourning,
Lo, the world in ashes burning.
Seer and Sybil gave the warning.
What shall I, frail man be pleading?

---

[92] Cf. Isaias xiii; Ezechiel x, xxii; Joel ii.

[93] St. Matthew xxiv, 29; Isaias xxiv, 19, 20; xxxiv, 4.

[94] Cf. St. Matthew xxiv, 29 ss.; St. Luke xxi, 25 ss.

[95] St. Luke xxi, 26.

[96] Cf. Isaias ii, 9.

Who for me be interceding
When the just are mercy needing?"

THE CHURCH FIRMLY ESTABLISHED

CHAPTER VII

1. After these things, I saw four angels standing on the four corners of the earth, holding the four winds of the earth that they should not blow upon the earth, nor upon the sea, nor on any tree.

2. And I saw another angel ascending from the rising of the sun, having the sign of the living God; and he cried with a loud voice to the four angels, to whom it was given to hurt the earth and the sea,

3. Saying: Hurt not the earth, nor the sea, nor the trees, till we sign the servants of our God in their foreheads.

4. And I heard the number of them that were signed, an hundred forty-four thousand were signed, of every tribe of the children of Israel.

5. Of the tribe of Juda were twelve thousand signed; of the tribe of Ruben, twelve thousand signed; of the tribe of Gad, twelve thousand signed;

6. Of the tribe of Aser, twelve thousand signed; of the tribe of Nephthali, twelve thousand signed; of the tribe of Manasses, twelve thousand signed.

7. Of the tribe of Simeon, twelve thousand signed; of the tribe of Levi, twelve thousand signed; of the tribe of Isaachar, twelve thousand signed:

8. Of the tribe of Zabulon, twelve thousand signed; of the tribe of Joseph, twelve thousand signed; of the tribe of Benjamin, twelve thousand signed.

This vision presages a period of comparative peace and security for the Church. By command of Christ the great persecutions are brought to an end that the Church may firmly establish herself upon the ruins of the old Roman Empire. Many Jews have accepted the teachings of Christ, and untold numbers from every race and tongue now flock to His standard.

1. The Apostle sees four spirits ready to send forth the winds of earth bearing persecution, war, pestilence, and famine. In the prophecy of Zacharias the four winds are four chariots bringing plagues upon earth.[97] They symbolize evil spirits and unfaithful pastors who bring untold harm to the faithful by their false teachings and example. The four horsemen of

---

[97] Zacharias vi, 1-5.

the preceding vision are here replaced by charioteers to signify that the threatened scourges are more grievous than any yet predicted.

2, 3. A faithful angel appears to prevent any injury to earth or sea until the servants of God are marked upon the forehead. This angel comes from the East to indicate that he has received his mission from Christ. Zacharias refers to the Messias as the Orient (the East.[98]) Hence it is Christ who brings persecution to an end that the Church may establish herself and spread the Gospel among Gentile peoples.

The office of this good angel is fulfilled by all bishops and priests, who by their teaching and example avert many evils. So today the teachings of the Church are the only remedy for the many ills that threaten society throughout the world. The nations must return to the Faith or perish from the earth.[99]

The strong voice is that of the Church which must resound unto the ends of the earth in preaching the Gospel. The sign upon the forehead represents the Sacraments of Baptism and Confirmation which imprint a spiritual mark upon the soul. In ancient times to be baptized was to be "signed." Confirmation was the "seal" of God's gifts.[100] As Confirmation was given immediately after Baptism, the two Sacraments are here represented by the one seal. In a secondary sense the cross is the sign imprinted upon the life of every true Christian. It is the "sign of the Son of man" which shall appear in the heavens at the second coming of Christ.[101]

4-8. Every tribe of Israel furnishes numerous converts to the Faith of Christ. This multitude of Jewish believers is represented by the symbolic number of 12,000 from each tribe. The Jews were not all unfaithful to the Messias. Many of them received the Gospel even in the days of the Apostles as we learn from the Acts of the Apostles and from the Epistles of St. Paul.

The tribe of Dan became so insignificant in numbers that it was never enumerated after the captivity. The number twelve was maintained by enumerating the two half -tribes of Manasses and Ephraim, sons of Joseph. Ephraim is here represented by Joseph.

---

[98] Zacharias vi, 12; St. Luke i, 78.

[99] Cf. Belloc, 'Europe and the Faith."

[100] Catholic Library, Archeology Series, vol. ii, pages 42, 43; cf. also Ephesians i, 13; iv, 30.

[101] St. Matthew xxiv, 30; cf. also Ezechiel ix, 4.

From this omission of Dan, St. Irenaeus concluded that Antichrist will spring from his tribe.[102] The prophecy of Jacob is cited in support of this belief: "Let Dan be a snake in the way; a serpent that biteth the horse's heels that the rider may fall backward."[103] This explanation of St. Irenaeus has but little to commend it because the tribes of Israel have long since lost their identity.

CHAPTER VII

9. After this I saw a great multitude which no man could number of all nations, and tribes, and peoples, and tongues, standing before the throne in the sight of the Lamb, clothed with white robes and palms in their hands

10. And they cried with a loud voice, saying: Salvation to our God who sitteth upon the throne, and to the Lamb.

11. And all the angels stood around about the throne, and the ancients and the four living creatures; and they fell down before the throne upon their faces and adored God.

12. Saying: Amen. Benediction and glory and wisdom, and thanksgiving, honor, and power, and strength to our God for ever and ever. Amen.

13. And one of the ancients answered, and said to me: These that are clothed in white robes, who are they? And whence came they?

14. And I said to him: My Lord, thou knowest. And he said to me: These are they who are come out of great tribulation, and have washed their robes and have made them white in the blood of the Lamb.

15. Therefore they are before the throne of God, and they serve him day and night in his temple: and he that sitteth on the throne shall dwell over them.

16. They shall no more hunger nor thirst, neither shall the sun fall on them, nor any heat.

17. For the Lamb, which is in the midst of the throne, shall rule them, .and shall lead them to the fountains of the waters of life, and God shall wipe away all tears from their eyes.

9. Many Jews accept the Gospel of Christ, but the Gentiles who flock to His fold from every nation and tongue form so vast a multitude that no man can number them. "There shall come from the east and the west, the

---

[102] St. Irenaeus, "Contra Haereses" xxx, 2.

[103] Genesis xlix, 17.

north and the south; and. shall sit down in the kingdom of God."[104] These elect shall be saved by purity of life symbolized by the white robes of innocence — an innocence obtained through the merits of Christ's death. Many shall also receive the glorious crown of martyrdom.

10-12. All join in one great hymn of praise and thanksgiving to God and to the Lamb who is worthy to receive divine honors.

With this vision persecutions cease; the Church comes forth triumphant from her long conflict with pagan Rome. A Christian now sits upon the throne of the Caesars; the Gospel is being preached far and wide and magnificent basilicas are being erected in which the liturgy of the Church is carried out with grand solemnity. The prophecy of Malachias is being fulfilled: "From the rising of the sun even to the going down, my name is great among the Gentiles, and in every place there is sacrifice and there is offered to my name a clean oblation: for my name is great among the Gentiles, saith the Lord of hosts."[105]

13-14. The faithful whom St. John beholds in the vision have passed through great tribulations. The era of persecution was a period of great tribulation for the whole Church as well as for those who actually suffered martyrdom.

Trials and tribulations shall frequently recur during the history of the Church as our Lord foretold: "If they have persecuted me they will also persecute you."[106] The most trying persecutions will be suffered in the days of Antichrist and at the end of the world.

The elect have washed their robes and made them white in the blood of the Lamb. They are saved by the merits of Christ's suffering and death, for "there is no other name under heaven given to men whereby we must be saved."[107]

15-17. Those who remain faithful to Christ, especially those who suffer for His sake, shall be rewarded in heaven for all their trials and sufferings on earth. There they shall be filled with all joy and consolation. "God shall wipe away all tears from their eyes; and death shall be no more, nor crying, nor sorrow."[108] Christ Himself shall rule over them all with an everlasting love.

---

[104] St. Luke xiii, 29.

[105] Malachias i, 11.

[106] St. John XV, 20.

[107] Acts of the Apostles iv, 12.

[108] Apocalypse xxi, 4

THE VICISSITUDES OF THE CHURCH

CHAPTER VIII

1. And when he had opened the seventh seal, there was silence in heaven, as it were for half an hour.

2. And I saw seven angels standing in the presence of God: and there were given to them seven trumpets.

3. Another angel came, and stood before the altar, having a golden censer; and there was given to him much incense, that he should offer of the prayers of all the saints upon the golden altar, which is before the throne of God.

4. And the smoke of the incense of the prayers of the saints ascended up before God from the hand of the angel.

5. And the angel took the censer, and filled it with the fire of the altar, and cast it on earth, and there were thunders and voices and lightnings, and a great earthquake.

6. And the seven angels, who had the seven trumpets, prepared themselves to sound the trumpet.

7. And the first angel sounded the trumpet, and there followed hail and fire, mingled with blood, and it was cast on the earth, and the third part of the earth was burnt up, and the third part of the trees was burnt up, and all green grass was burnt up.

The breaking of the seventh seal reveals the vicissitudes of the Church during the centuries which follow its establishment upon the ruins of the Roman Empire. The varying fortunes of the Church during these centuries serve to separate the good from the bad. This work of separation goes on through all the centuries to be completed only at the last judgment. Hence the visions of the seventh seal continue on to the end of the Apocalypse.

We can now begin to realize how logically the prophecies of the Apocalypse are developed. Each succeeding chapter presents in regular order a new period of the Church's existence on earth.

1. Upon the breaking of the seventh seal there is silence in heaven, — a mark of reverence and awe. The half hour represents the time given St. John to contemplate the vision set before him.

2. The seven angels before the throne of God are ever ready to execute His commands for "are they not all ministering spirits?"[109] Seven, the perfect number, signifies the thoroughness with which God's every command shall be carried into effect. In a symbolic meaning these angels represent the bishops and the priests of the Church. Each one is given a trumpet to proclaim the Gospel to the uttermost bounds of the earth. The voice shall be clear and strong, leaving no excuse for those who will not hear.

3, 4. Another angel offers to God the prayers of the faithful on the golden altar of incense. The prayers are symbolized by the sweet odors rising up before the throne of God. St. John takes much of his symbolism from the tabernacle and from the Temple of Jerusalem.

During the wanderings of the Israelites in the wilderness, the tabernacle furnished them a miniature representation of the court of heaven. In the Holy of Holies stood the ark of the covenant overshadowed by the outstretched wings of two cherubim. The lid of the ark was considered the throne of God who there dwelt amongst His people. Before the throne, but separated from it by a veil, stood the golden altar of incense in the Holy Place. Here the priests daily offered incense which arose before God as a sweet odor to symbolize the prayers of the people: "Let my prayer be directed as incense in thy sight."[110]

The tabernacle, — the earthly representation of the heavenly court, — was reproduced in the temple of Jerusalem which thus became "the pattern of heavenly things" as St. Paul says. Again he writes: "Jesus is not entered into the Holies made with hands, the patterns of the true; but into heaven itself."[111] Hence it is most appropriate for St. John to use the temple as a figure of the Church which is truly the dwelling place of God, the heavenly court on earth.

The incense offered by the angel at the golden altar of incense symbolizes the prayers of the faithful, and especially the holy sacrifice of the Mass offered to God through the ministry of the priesthood represented here, as elsewhere, by the angel. The altar of incense, and the altar of holocaust mentioned in vi, 9, probably symbolize Christ who offered Himself "a propitiation for our sins: and not for ours only, but also for

---

[109] Hebrews i, 14.

[110] Psalm cxl, 2.

[111] Hebrews ix, 23, 24.

those of the whole world," and is "always living to make intercession for us."[112]

5. The fire taken from the altar symbolizes the merits of Christ which give value to all our works and prayers, as the fire kindles the incense and sends forth its sweet perfumes. The fire is cast upon earth; in other words the merits of Christ are offered to the unfaithful who reject them and thus bring down the punishments of God, — thunders, lightnings, and earthquakes. A similar punishment is predicted below in verse 7.

6. The seven angels preparing to sound their trumpets represent the bishops and priests of the Church going forth to preach the Gospel to every creature. Their voice shall resound through the world like a trumpet-blast. Christ said to His Apostles: "That which I tell you in the dark, speak ye in the light; and that which you hear in the ear, preach ye upon the house-tops."[113]

7. Some will hearken to the voice of Christ in the preaching of His Gospel. Others will harden their hearts and refuse to obey. These shall be chastised by fire from heaven to destroy their harvests. The fire is mingled with blood, — a symbol of war and revolutions. Here is fulfilled the prophecy of the aged Simeon: "Behold, this child set for the fall, and for the resurrection of many in Israel, and for a sign which shall be contradicted."[114]

According to St. Irenaeus, plagues similar to those of Egypt in the days of Moses shall afflict all unfaithful nations in the days of Antichrist.[115]

CHAPTER VIII

8. *And the second angel sounded the trumpet; and as it were a great mountain, burning with fire, was cast into the sea, and the third part of the sea became blood:*

9. *And the third part of those creatures died, which had life in the sea, and the third part of the ships was destroyed.*

10. *And the third angel sounded the trumpet, and a great star fell from heaven, burning, as it were, a torch, and it fell on the third part of the rivers, and upon the fountains of waters:*

---

[112] I John ii, 2; Hebrews vii, 25.

[113] St. Matthew x, 27.

[114] St. Luke ii, 34.

[115] St Irenaeus, "Adversus Haereses" IV, 30, iv; cf. also Apocalypse xvi.

11. And the name of the star is called Wormwood. And the third part of the waters became wormwood; and many men died of the waters, because they were made bitter.

12. And the fourth angel sounded the trumpet, and the third part of the sun was smitten, and the third part of the moon, and the third part of the stars, so that the third part of them was darkened and the day did not shine for a third part of it, and the night in like manner.

13. And I beheld, and heard the voice of one eagle flying through the midst of heaven, saying with a loud voice: Woe, woe, woe to the inhabitants of the earth: by reason of the rest of the voices of the three angels, who are yet to sound the trumpet.

8. At the sound of the second trumpet a burning mountain, or volcano, is hurled into the sea thereby changing a third part of the waters to blood. In Holy Scripture a mountain symbolizes a powerful nation or government.[116] As usual the sea represents human society. The vision shows that despite the preaching of the Gospel some great nation will bring war and bloodshed upon a large portion of mankind. It also predicts great persecutions against the Church. Nations will seek to destroy the Church at all hazards. This double interpretation is fully confirmed by the history of the past and present.

9. The fish are the faithful scattered amongst the people of the world. The ships are churches of the various nations. In the early ages the fish was a common symbol of Christ and of the faithful, as the ship was a figure of the Church.[117] Numberless Christians and even whole churches have often perished in wars and persecutions. And only too often have the weaker brethren denied their Faith through fear of torture and death.

10. As the third angel sounds his trumpet a great star falls from heaven like a flaming torch and poisons a large portion of the streams and even their very sources. The name wormwood denotes a bitter and poisonous nature. This vision is a striking image of unfaithful bishops and priests who fall from the firmament of the Church where Christ has placed them to enlighten and direct the world. By false teachings and example they poison the very sources of doctrine which should flow pure as water from the

---

[116] Cf. Jeremias li, 25; Zacharias iv, 7.

[117] Catholic Library, Archaeology Series, voi ii. page 83.

mountain torrent. Like our divine Savior, the bishops and priests of the Church must be "fountains of water springing up into life everlasting."[118]

11. Unfortunately many of the faithful drink from these poisoned streams of false doctrine and so perish.

12. The thoughts of many hearts are being revealed more and more as the Gospel is preached throughout the world.[119] Many reject it; others abandon it. There is a growing decadence in the Church. Its doctrine and sanctity shine with diminished luster. The day is less brilliant; the night of ignorance becomes darker. This is symbolized by the darkening of the sun, moon and stars. In such critical times in the past God has always raised up illustrious saints and religious orders to awaken the zeal and strengthen the faith of His people. He will most assuredly do likewise in the future for He said: "Behold, I am with you all days even to the consummation of the world."[120] Many a time our Lord seems to sleep as the bark of His Church is beaten by the storm- tossed sea. In His own good time He arises to command the waves: Peace be still.[121]

The prophecies of this chapter have been fulfilled many times in the past. No doubt they will often be verified in the future. It should be noted, however, that a progressive accumulation of evils is predicted. At first it affects individuals only (v. 7). Then a nation or an entire church is involved (v. 8), and a number of great heretics fall away from the Faith (v. 10). Finally the whole Church suffers from a weakening of Faith and discipline (v. 12). This gradual progression of evil, this "mystery of iniquity" which was working even in the days of St. Paul,[122] will finally usher in the Antichrist.

13. An eagle appears in mid-heaven proclaiming three great woes to follow the sounding of the remaining trumpets. Two interpretations are permissible. The first recognizes in the eagle a powerful nation which shall be an instrument of God's judgments upon the world. The other interpretation sees in the eagle a symbol of new preachers of the Gospel. God raises up new saints or religious orders to arouse the faithful to

---

[118] St. John iv, 14.

[119] St. Luke ii, 35.

[120] St. Matthew xxviii, 20.

[121] St. Luke viii, 23, 24.

[122] II Thessalonians ii, 7.

renewed faith and zeal in His service. Nevertheless, three great evils shall afflict the Church before her final victory over the world and the devil.

Whatever interpretation be adopted, there can be no doubt that this verse heralds the beginning of a new and important epoch in the history of the Church.

PART II: From the Opening of the Abyss to Its Closing

And I saw a star fall from heaven upon the earth, and there was given to him the keg of the bottomless pit. And he opened the bottomless pit.

APOCALYPSE
ix, 1, 2,

HERESIES AND RELIGIOUS WARS

CHAPTER IX

1. And the fifth angel sounded the trumpet, and I saw a star fall from heaven upon the earth, and there was given to him the key of the bottomless pit.

2. And he opened the bottomless pit: and the smoke of the pit arose, as the smoke of a great furnace: and the sun and the air were darkened with the smoke of the pit.

3. And from the smoke of the pit there came out locusts upon the earth. And power was given to them, as the scorpions of the earth have power:

4. And it was commanded them that they should not hurt the grass of the earth, nor any green thing, nor any tree; But only the men who have not the sign of God on their foreheads

5. And it was given unto them that they should not kill them; but that they should torment them five months: And their torment was as the torment of a scorpion when he striketh a man.

6. And in those days men shall seek death, and shall not find it: and they shall desire to die, and death shall fly from them.

7. And the shapes of the locusts were like unto horses prepared unto battle: and on their heads were, as it were crowns like gold: and their faces were as the faces of men.

8. And they had hair as the hair of women; and their teeth were as lions:

9. And they had breastplates as breastplates of iron, and the noise of their wings was as the noise of chariots and many horses running to battle.

10. And they had tails like to scorpions, and there were stings in their tails; and their power was to hurt men five months. And they had over them

11. A king, the angel of the bottomless pit; whose name in Hebrew is Abaddon, and in Greek Apollyon; in Latin Exterminans.

The vision described in this chapter is one of the most important of the whole Apocalypse. It foretells the first woe announced by the flying eagle, — the conditions and events destined to usher in the reign of Antichrist.

1. In the fallen star ancient commentators saw a figure of Arius and other early heretics. As a matter of fact, any priest or bishop of the Church who

becomes the leader of heresy may be compared to a star fallen from heaven. But in this case the star refers to some particular person whose revolt from the Church shall lead directly to the reign of Antichrist.

We cannot agree with those who refer the beginning of this vision to the early ages of the Church. The prophecies of St. John are developed in regular order according to time This vision marks a new period of exceptional gravity for the Church. We hold with Cornelius a Lapide and many others that it refers to the pretended Reformation with the star as a symbol of Luther. In that case the fifth angel may be taken as a figure of the defenders of Catholic Faith in those days.

The Arian heresy and the Greek schism had deplorable results for the Church, but they cannot be compared to those of the religious upheaval of the sixteenth century. Most of the evils that afflict the Church and society in general can be traced directly to the so-called Reformation. To it must be ascribed the apostasy of nations, the weakening of faith, and the rapidly increasing impiety and unbelief of the present day. As a result of these evils great social disturbances appear on every side, and society is tottering to its very foundations. The reign of Antichrist, which must be relatively near, will mark the culmination of evil.

2. Instead of the "keys of heaven" this apostate priest received the "key of the bottomless pit." He did in very truth open the pit by turning loose against the Church all the fury of hell. By tongue and pen he instilled into the hearts of individuals and nations a diabolic hatred of the Church which still manifests itself in calumny, misrepresentation and opposition to the Church.

The dense smoke arising from the pit obscures the heavens. This signifies that the heresy shall succeed for a time. True Catholic doctrine is obscured and even lost to many peoples.

3. From the smoke of the pit comes forth a swarm of locusts. Unlike ordinary locusts they attack men instead of growing plants. In this respect they have the power or nature of scorpions. These locusts are a fitting image of demons, heretics, and apostates who swarm over the earth spreading spiritual destruction far and wide.

4, 5. These verses make it clear that there is no question of real locusts such as those that ravaged Egypt in the days of Moses. They are purely symbolic, and their ravages chiefly spiritual. Their sting burns and poisons the soul with false doctrines, but has no power to injure those who remain faithful to the graces received in Baptism and Confirmation. For a short time these locusts are permitted to harass and persecute without killing, but they cannot destroy the Church.

6. In those days men seek death and find it not. The good would welcome death as an escape from the evils and miseries that surround them. Many who have been led astray by false doctrines would likewise welcome death as a relief from their doubts and remorse of conscience.

7. The locusts resemble horses accoutered for war. Heresy and schism are ever fruitful sources of religious wars and persecutions. The crowns indicate that rulers, — emperors, kings, and princes will be arrayed against the Church as actually happened at the Reformation in the sixteenth century. The crowns merely resembled gold, because there was but a mere semblance of real Christian charity in those days. The human faces prove that these locusts symbolize real persons.

8-10. The hair of a woman probably signifies vanity and immorality; the teeth of a lion strength and cruelty. The breastplates of iron show preparedness for defense as well as for attack. The sound of their innumerable wings resembles the thunder of chariots rushing to battle. This indicates their great numbers and impetuosity. The scorpion-like sting is a symbol of heresy that stings and poisons the soul. Its location in the tail signifies deceit and hypocrisy.[123]

11. The king of these symbolic locusts is called the Destroyer (Exterminans). He is Lucifer, the angel of the abyss, the leader of the rebel angels. His minions on earth are the leaders of heresy, schism, and persecution.

CHAPTER IX

12. One woe is past, and behold there come yet two woes more hereafter.

13. And the sixth angel sounded the trumpet: and I heard a voice from the four horns of the golden altar, which is before the eyes of God,

14. Saying to the sixth angel, who had the trumpet: Loose the four angels, who are bound in the great river Euphrates.

15. And the four angels were loosed, who were prepared for an hour, and a day, and a month, and a year: for to kill the third part of men.

16. And the number of the army of horsemen was twenty thousand times ten thousand. And I heard the number of them.

---

[123] See below, verse 19.

17. And thus I saw the horses in the vision: and they that sat on them, had breastplates of fire and of hyacinth and of brimstone, and the heads of the horses were as the heads of lions: and from their mouths proceeded fire, and smoke, and brimstone.

18. And by these three plagues was slain the third part of men, by the fire and by the smoke and by the brimstone, which issued out of their mouths.

19. For the power of the horses is in their mouths, and in their tails. For, their tails are like to serpents, and have heads: and with them they hurt.

20. And the rest of the men, who were not slain by these plagues, did not do penance from the works of their hands, that they should not adore devils, and idols of gold, and silver, and brass, and stone, and wood, which neither can see, nor hear, nor walk.

21. Neither did they penance from their murders, nor from their sorceries, nor from their fornication, nor from their thefts.

12. The invasion of the locusts is the first woe predicted by the eagle. The two yet to come will fill up the "mystery of iniquity" with the appearance of Antichrist and his prophet.

13. God sends a sixth angel to instruct and guide the Church. This mission will still further reveal the thoughts of many hearts. The wicked continue to be separated from the just.

A voice from the golden altar commands the captive angels of the Euphrates to be released. As noted above, the altar is Christ, who makes trials and tribulations a means of sanctification for souls and an increase of fervor and holiness in the Church. They also serve to spread the blessings of the Gospel for as Tertullian says: "The blood, of martyrs is the seed of Christians."[124]

Christ Himself gives command to release the captive angels, thus showing that the enemies of the Church have no power against her unless God permits. The Church can say to her enemies as Christ said to Pilate: "Thou shouldst not have any power against me, unless it were given thee from above."[125]

14. The captive angels are demons who will arouse new enemies and increased enmities against the Church. In a figurative sense they represent the new enemies thus aroused against the Church, whether they be nations,

---

[124] Tertullian, "Apology" c. 50

[125] St. John xix, 11.

70

individuals or secret societies hostile to her. Four, the number of universality, indicates how widespread will be their influence.

With the prophets of old the region of the Euphrates was ever the country whence came the enemies of God's people. Its mention here indicates that these new enemies will arise among nations already hostile to the Church. In a secondary sense the term may be taken literally to represent peoples from that region who are hostile to the Church.

The four angels of the Euphrates, now ordered to be released, may be the same as those whom Christ forbade to injure the earth until the Church could be firmly established after the persecutions.[126]

15. Even the time for the manifestation of these evil spirits and their minions has been accurately fixed in the designs of Providence. The very day and hour has been determined.

Great numbers will be done to death in the religious wars and revolutions stirred up by these angels from the Euphrates. The prophecy may also mean that large numbers will be led into new errors and schisms. Both interpretations are fully justified by the history of the pretended Reformation and the wars that followed it.

16. These scourges shall be more terrible than any yet predicted. The first plagues were brought to earth by four horsemen (ch. vi). Then we saw four charioteers, the four winds, ready to scourge mankind. Here we find a vast array of cavalry. The chastisements sent upon the world increase with the growth of iniquity and the approach of Antichrist.

17, 18. The description of horses and riders in this vision gives some idea of their boldness, strength, and cunning ferocity. They inflict upon men the plagues of fire, smoke and sulphur. The fire is persecution and war. Smoke symbolizes the obscuring of doctrine and the weakening of faith; sulphur, the moral depravity which follows.

The fire, smoke and sulphur issue from the mouth of the horses. From the mouth should proceed words of wisdom; instead there come forth heresies, and incitements to revolt and revolution. It should be noted that Luther openly preached revolt and revolution to the peasants of Germany, but when they put his words into practice, he turned to the princes and urged them to stamp out the revolt with fire and sword.

19. The horses of this vision inflict injuries with their tails which resemble serpents. Amongst all peoples the serpent is a symbol of lying

---

[126] See above, vii, 1.

and hypocrisy. These vices have ever characterized the enemies of the Church.

There is no question here of real artillery as some have imagined. St. John is giving only the broad outlines of the Church's history. He is not concerned with the material means employed by men to wage war against her.

The vision of locusts and the vision of cavalry horses are not two representations of one and the same event. They foreshadow two distinct events that follow one another in the order of time. The one is the great revolt against the Church brought about by the fallen star. The other consists of wars and disturbances which follow in the wake of that revolt.

20, 21. After these plagues have passed there still remain many who worship idols, and many guilty of robbery, murder, and immorality. This is verified today. Although nineteen twenty have elapsed since the first preaching of the Gospel, whole nations are still steeped in idolatry, and Christendom seems hopelessly divided by heresy and schism. Man's obstinacy in evil brings on the plagues described in subsequent chapters.

A PREPARATORY VISION

CHAPTER X

1. And I saw another mighty angel come down from heaven, clothed with a cloud, and a rainbow was on his head, and his face was as the sun, and his feet as pillars of fire.

2. And he had in his hand a little book open: and he set his right foot upon the sea, and his left foot upon the earth.

3. And he cried with a loud voice as when a lion roareth. And when he had cried seven thunders uttered their voices.

4. And when the seven thunders had uttered their voices, I was about to write: and I heard a voice from heaven saying to me: Seal up the things which the seven thunders have spoken, and write them not.

5. And the angel whom I saw standing upon the sea and upon the earth, lifted up his hand to heaven.

6. And swore by him that liveth for ever and ever, who created heaven, and the things which are therein; and the earth, and the things which are in it; and the sea, and the things which are therein; That time shall be no longer.

7. But in the days of the voice of the seventh angel, when he shall begin to sound the trumpet, the mystery of God shall be finished, as he hath declared by his servants, the prophets.

1. An angel coming in clouds of grace and glory brings to St. John a book of further prophecies. The rainbow about his head symbolizes mercy,[127] while the brightness of his countenance expresses the power of his teachings to enlighten souls. The feet as of fire indicate that he shall lead the Church in the ways of truth and justice as the pillar of fire guided the Israelites in the wilderness.[128]

2. The book is open to signify that the prophecies therein revealed to St. John are intelligible and shall be understood in due time according to the

---

[127] See above.

[128] Exodus xiii, 21.

needs of the Church. The angel places one foot upon the sea, the other upon the land to express God's supreme dominion over all things.

3, 4. The voice like the roar of a lion is the voice of the Gospel which shall penetrate to the very ends of the earth teaching divine truth, condemning error, and threatening persecutors with the vengeance of God. Here, as elsewhere, the thunders may symbolize the anathemas of the Church against all wickedness and error; but it would be useless to comment on their exact meaning since St. John was commanded to seal up their words. In like manner Daniel was ordered to seal up the words of his prophecies until the time appointed by God for their publication.[129] The words of the seven thunders may also have been such as St. Paul heard — "secret words which it is not granted to man to utter."[130]

5, 6. Lifting his hand to heaven the angel calls upon the God of all creation to witness the truth of his words that time shall be no more. This does not mean that the end of the world is at hand, but that the time for judgment against obstinate sinners and persecutors has arrived.

7. This judgment shall be the great persecution of Antichrist and its attendant evils. Then shall be accomplished the "mystery of God" which has been announced (evangelized) by the prophets of old. To evangelize is to announce good tidings, hence this "mystery of God" is probably the plenitude of the Redemption applied to all nations of earth. After the destruction of Antichrist and his kingdom all peoples shall accept the Gospel and the Church of Christ shall reign peacefully over all nations.[131]

CHAPTER X

8. *And I heard a voice from heaven again speaking to me, and saying: Go, and take the book that is open, from the hand of the angel who standeth upon the sea, and upon the earth.*

9. *And I went to the angel, saying unto him, that he should give me the book. And he said to me: Take the book, and eat it up: and it shall make thy belly bitter but in thy mouth it shall be sweet as honey.*

10. *And I took the book from the hand of the angel, and ate it up: and it was in my mouth sweet as honey: and when I had eaten it, my belly was bitter.*

---

[129] Daniel xii, 4.

[130] II Corinthians xii, 4.

[131] See below, "Universal Reign of Christ."

11. And he said to me: Thou must prophecy again to many nations, and peoples, and tongues, and kings.

8-10. Eating the book symbolizes an intimate union with the Holy Ghost by which the mind of the Apostle is illuminated with the spirit of prophecy. St. John finds the book sweet to the taste because it announces mercy to the elect and the final triumph of the Church. It is bitter in so far as it predicts dire persecution for the Church and terrible punishment for the wicked.

11. The angel commands St. John to announce to all the prophecy communicated to him concerning the reign of Antichrist, the subsequent triumph of the Church, and the final persecution under Gog and Magog.

THE TWO WITNESSES

CHAPTER XI

1. And there was given to me a reed like unto a rod: and it was said to me: Arise, and measure the temple of God, and the altar and them that adore therein.

2. But the court, which is without the temple, cast out, and measure it not: because it is given unto the Gentiles, and the holy city they shall tread under foot two and forty months.

3. And I will give unto my two witnesses, and they shall prophesy a thousand two hundred sixty days, clothed in sackcloth.

4. These are the two olive trees, and the two candlesticks, that stand before the Lord of the earth.

5. And if any man will hurt them, fire shall come out of their mouths, and shall devour their enemies. And if any man will hurt them, in this manner must he be slain.

6. These have power to shut heaven, that it rain not in the days of their prophecy: and they have power over waters to turn them into blood, and to strike the earth with all plagues as often as they will.

7. And when they shall have finished their testimony, the beast, that ascendeth out of the abyss, shall make war against them, and overcome them, and kill them.

8. And their bodies shall lie in the streets of the great city, which is called spiritually, Sodom and Egypt, where their Lord also was crucified.

9. And they of the tribes, and peoples, and tongues, and nations, shall see their bodies for three days and a half: and they shall not suffer their bodies to be laid in sepulchres.

10. And they that dwell upon the earth shall rejoice over them, and make merry: and shall send gifts one to another, because these two prophets tormented them that dwelt upon earth.

11. And after three days and a half, the spirit of life from God entered into them. And they stood upon their feet, and great fear fell upon them that saw them.

12. And they heard a great voice from heaven, saying to them: Come up hither. And they went up to heaven in a cloud: and their enemies saw them.

13. And at that hour there was a great earthquake, and the tenth part of the city fell: and there were slain in the earthquake names of men seven thousand: and the rest were cast into a fear, and gave glory to the God of heaven.

The account of the two witnesses given here in one connected discourse, necessitates a brief outline of the reign of Antichrist, his persecution of the Church, and his overwhelming defeat, — events to be more fully related in subsequent chapters.

1. St. John is commanded to measure the temple and number the people found therein. Here again, the temple is a figure of the Church and those who worship there are the faithful who remain steadfast during the great persecution of Antichrist.

2. The outer court, cast off and given over to the Gentiles, signifies that a great number of Christians will fall away from the Faith in those evil days. With the other followers of Antichrist they will trample Jerusalem beneath their feet during the forty-two months of persecution. The holy city is here taken literally for Jerusalem, but it is also a figure of the Church, the chief object of attack under Antichrist.

3. At the beginning of this terrible persecution God will send two prophets, or "witnesses," to guide the Church and preach penance for the space of 1260 days. According to all tradition, both Jewish and Christian, the prophet Elias, will be one of these witnesses. "Behold I will send you Elias the prophet, before the coming of the great day of the Lord."[132] The tradition is also confirmed by the words of Christ: "Elias indeed shall come and restore all things."[133] The other witness will probably be Henoch, who like Elias, "was translated that he should not see death."[134] Yet some think that Moses will be the second witness because he appeared with Elias at the Transfiguration of Christ.[135] The two witnesses shall appear among men as apostles of the Church and adversaries of Antichrist.

The duration of the persecution is sometimes given in years; at other times in months or days, but in every case the same definite length of time

---

[132] Malachias iv, 5.

[133] St. Matthew xvii, 11.

[134] IV Kings ii, 3; Epistle to Hebrews xi, 5.

[135] St. Matthew xvii, 3.

is predicted. This seems to indicate that the three and one-half years are to be taken literally.

4. The two witnesses were symbolized by the two olive trees and the candlestick mentioned in the prophecy of Zacharias.[136] The olive is a symbol of God's mercy as in the days of the deluge.[137] The oil from the olive also symbolizes the unction of the Holy Ghost poured forth upon the two prophets who are to be lights (candlesticks) to the faithful by their preaching.

5, 6. The two witnesses shall have miraculous power to overcome their enemies as Elias of old destroyed the soldiers of Ochozias with fire from heaven.[138] They shall also punish the unfaithful with drought and famine as did Elias in the days of Achab.[139] Changing water into blood may mean that the rivers shall run red with blood from wars and revolutions. More probably the words should be taken literally to foretell plagues such as Moses brought upon the land of Egypt.[140] In either case there is a reference to the plagues of Egypt which seems to confirm the belief that Moses shall be one of the witnesses.

7. Having fulfilled their mission the two prophets will be put to death by Antichrist, — the beast from the abyss.[141] Thus will they share the fate of their divine Master and of innumerable heralds of the Gospel. Their martyrdom will take place at the end of a war in which Antichrist and his followers will win the decisive battle in the vicinity of Jerusalem.

8-10. For three days and. a half the bodies of the martyred prophets shall lie unburied in the streets of Jerusalem "where our Lord was crucified." The enemies of the Church will rejoice and commemorate their short-lived victory by exchange of gifts. Like the Jews of old who thought they had rid themselves of Christ by His death on the Cross, these enemies of His Church will think they have done with the prophets who harassed them by their preaching and miracles. Naturally, the faithful will be seized with fear, as were the disciples at the death of our Lord.

---

[136] Zacharias iv, 3.

[137] Genesis viii, 11.

[138] IV Kings i, 10-14.

[139] III Kings xvii, 1.

[140] Exodus vii, 20 ss.

[141] See below, xiii, 1.

11, 12. At the end of three days and a half the followers of Antichrist shall be dumbfounded to see the two prophets arise from the dead and ascend into heaven before their very eyes.

Centuries before, Elias and Henoch had been taken up from earth[142] and reserved for this supreme conflict. Now by a special privilege they anticipate the general resurrection as a reward for their labors and sufferings.

This triumph of the two prophets leads directly to the defeat of Antichrist as foretold by Isaias: "With the breath of his lips shall he slay the wicked one."[143] In like manner St. Paul says: "Then that wicked one shall be revealed whom the Lord Jesus shall kill with the spirit of His mouth."[144] These passages seem to imply a personal intervention by our Lord but He may send an angel as His instrument of destruction; or, perhaps, Elias will rain down fire from heaven upon Antichrist as he did upon the soldiers of Ochozias and the priests of Baal.[145]

13. As the two prophets are taken up to heaven Jerusalem is shaken with a mighty earthquake in which seven thousand people perish and a tenth part of the city is destroyed. At sight of these prodigies all who survive are converted and begin to praise and glorify God. Here is seen the great mercy of God who punishes not to destroy but to convert and save.

CHAPTER XI

14. And the second woe is past: And behold the third woe will come quickly.

15. And the seventh angel sounded the trumpet: and there were great voices in heaven, saying: The kingdom of this world is become our Lord's and his Christ's, and he shall reign for ever and ever, Amen.

16. And the four and twenty ancients, who sit on their seats in the sight of God, fell on their faces and adored God, saying:

17. We give thee thanks, O Lord God Almighty, who art, and who wast, and who art to come: because thou hast taken to thee thy great power, and thou hast reigned.

---

[142] Genesis v, 22; Eccli xlvii, 9, 10; IV King's ii, 11; Hebrews xi, 5.

[143] Isaias xi, 4.

[144] II Thessalonians ii, 8.

[145] III Kings xvii, 38-40; IV Kings i, 10-14; cf. below, xiv, 18.

18. And the nations were angry, and thy wrath is come, and the time of the dead, that they should be judged and that thou shouldst render reward to thy servants the prophets and the saints, and to them that fear thy name, little and great, and shouldst destroy them who have corrupted the earth.

19. And the temple of God was opened in heaven: and the ark of his testament was seen in his temple, and there were lightnings, and voices, and an earthquake, and great hail.

14. The reign of Antichrist is the second woe announced by the eagle.[146] The third woe following close upon the second shall end with the destruction of Rome, the new Babylon,[147] and the defeat of the false prophet.

15. The seventh angel proclaims the triumph of Christ and His kingdom which shall endure until the end of time. The Church, the kingdom of Christ, shall be established upon the ruins of the empire of Antichrist far more gloriously than it had been upon the ruins of the old empire of pagan Rome. Heresies, schisms and religious wars shall be no more, and all nations shall be converted to Christianity.

16, 17. The paeans of the four and twenty ancients to their triumphant Savior represent the praises of the Church given to Christ through the ministry of the priesthood.

18. Toward the end of the world a final revolt against the Church shall be punished by a deluge of fire.[148] Shortly thereafter shall come the resurrection of the body, and the general judgment in which God will reward His prophets and saints, and all who fear His name be they great or small. The wicked shall then suffer the just punishment of their iniquity.

19. If this verse be connected with the foregoing, it describes the intervention of Christ to protect His Church against her enemies in the last conflict at the end of the world. It seems better, however, to take it as a prelude to the following chapter. It then refers to the assistance which God gives His Church in her conflict with Satan mentioned above (vv. 2, 3), and described at length in the following chapters.

The ark of the testament is the Eucharistic Tabernacle in which Christ dwells with His Church. The lightnings, voices, and earthquake (thunders,

---

[146] Apocalypse viii, 13.

[147] Apocalypse xviii.

[148] Apocalypse xx.

in Greek) symbolize the preaching and warnings of the Church; her anathemas and judgments against all heresy and schism, and the divine punishment which these sins bring down upon those guilty of them.

CONFLICT BETWEEN THE CHURCH AND SATAN

CHAPTER XII

1. And a great sign appeared in heaven: A woman clothed with the sun, and the moon under her feet, and on her head a crown of twelve stars:

2. And being with child, she cried travailing in birth and was in pain to be delivered.

3. And there was seen another sign in heaven: and behold a great red dragon, having seven heads, and ten horns: and on his heads seven diadems:

4. And his tail drew the third part of the stars of heaven, and cast them to the earth: and the dragon stood before the woman who was ready to be delivered; that, when she should be delivered, he might devour her son.

5. And she brought forth a man child, who was to rule all nations with an iron rod: and her son was taken up to God and to his throne.

6. And the woman fled into the wilderness, where she had a place prepared by God, that there they should feed her a thousand two hundred sixty days.

7. And there was a great battle in heaven, Michael and his angels fought with the dragon, and the dragon fought and his angels.

8. And they prevailed not, neither was their place found any more in heaven.

9. And that great dragon was cast out, that old serpent who is called the devil and Satan, who seduceth the whole world: and he was cast unto earth, and his angels were thrown down with him.

In the foregoing chapter St. John outlines the history of the Church from the coming of Antichrist until the end of the world in order to give a connected account of the two prophets Elias and Henoch, (or Moses) and the result of their labors. In this chapter he shows us the true nature of that conflict. It shall be war unto death between the Church and the powers of darkness in a final effort of Satan to destroy the Church and thus prevent the universal reign of Christ on earth.

Satan will first attempt to destroy the power of the Papacy and bring about the downfall of the Church through heresies, schisms and persecutions that must surely follow. Failing in this he will then attack the Church from without. For this purpose he will raise up Antichrist and his prophet to lead the faithful into error and destroy those who remain steadfast.

1. The Church, the faithful spouse of Jesus Christ, is represented as a woman clothed in the glory of divine grace. In the Canticle of Canticles the Church is likewise described as "she that cometh forth as the morning rising, fair as the moon, bright as the sun."[149] The brightness of the sun is a fitting symbol for the enlightening power of the Church's teachings.

The moon was beneath her feet. St. Gregory the Great and St. Augustine see in this the dominion of the Church over the whole world, and her contempt for the perishable goods of this life. The moon with its ever changing phases is a figure of the transitory things of earth.

The crown of twelve stars represents the twelve Apostles and through them the whole ministry of the Church. It may also denote the assembly of faithful nations symbolized by the mystic number twelve.

2. The Church is ever in labor to bring forth children to eternal life. In the sad days here predicted the sorrows and pains of delivery shall be increased many fold. In this passage there is, an evident allusion to some particular son of the Church whose power and influence shall be such that Satan will seek his destruction at any cost. This person can be none other than the Pope to be elected in those days. The Papacy will be attacked by all the powers of hell. In consequence the Church will suffer great trials and afflictions in securing a successor upon the throne of Peter.

The words of St. Paul to the Thessalonians may be a reference to the Papacy as the obstacle to the coming of Antichrist: "You know what withholdeth, that he may be revealed in his time. For the mystery of iniquity already worketh; only that he who now holdeth, do hold, until he be taken out of the way. And then that wicked one shall be revealed."[150]

3. St. John now sees in heaven a red dragon with seven heads and ten horns; each head bearing a diadem. The dragon is Satan red with the blood of martyrs which he will cause to flow. The meaning of the seven heads and ten horns must be sought in the description of the beast that represents Antichrist where they symbolize kings or worldly powers.[151] Those of the

---

[149] Canticle of Canticles vi, 9.

[150] II Thessalonians ii, 6, 7.

[151] Apocalypse xvii, 9-12.

dragon must have a similar meaning, and indicate that Satan's attacks against the Church will be organized and carried out by the governments and ruling powers of those days.

With the beast of Antichrist only the horns have diadems as symbols of royalty or governing power. The heads are branded with names of blasphemy.[152] Hence they symbolize the sins and errors that will afflict the Church. Seven, the number of universality, indicates that in this final struggle to prevent the universal reign of Christ all forms of sin and error will be marshalled against the Church. A prelude to this may be seen in the errors of Modernism which has been rightly designated "a synthesis of all heresies." The number seven is also appropriate since all sins are included in the seven capital sins. In like manner all errors that have afflicted the Church may be summed up in these seven: Judaism, paganism, Arianism, Mohammedanism, Protestantism, rationalism, and atheism.

The dragon is seen in heaven which is here a symbol of the Church, the kingdom of heaven on earth. This indicates that the first troubles of those days will be inaugurated within the Church by apostate bishops, priests, and peoples, — the stars dragged down by the tail of the dragon.

4. The tail of the dragon represents the cunning hypocrisy with which he succeeds in deceiving a large number of people and pastors — a third part of the stars. Arianism led away many bishops, priests and peoples. The pretended Reformation of the sixteenth century claimed still larger numbers but these cannot be compared to the numbers seduced by Satan in the days of Antichrist.

The dragon stands before the woman ready to devour the child that is brought forth. In other words, the powers of hell seek by all means to destroy the Pope elected in those days.

5. The woman brings forth a son to rule the nations with a rod of iron. These are the identical words of prophecy uttered by the Psalmist concerning our Savior Jesus Christ.[153] They confirm our application of this vision to the Pope, the vicar of Christ on earth to rule the nations in His stead and by His power.

It is now the hour for the powers of darkness. The new-born Son of the Church is taken "to God and to His throne." Scarcely has the newly elected Pope been enthroned when he is snatched away by martyrdom. The

---

[152] Apocalypse xiii, 1.

[153] Psalm ii, 9.

"mystery of iniquity" gradually developing through the centuries, cannot be fully consummated while the power of the Papacy endures, but now he that "withholdeth is taken out of the way." During the interregnum "that wicked one shall be revealed" in his fury against the Church.

It is a matter of history that the most disastrous periods for the Church were times when the Papal throne was vacant, or when anti-popes contended with the legitimate head of the Church. Thus also shall it be in those evil days to come.

6. The Church deprived of her chief pastor must seek sanctuary in solitude there to be guided by God Himself during those trying days. This place of refuge prepared for the Church is probably some nation, or nations, that remain faithful to her.[154] In those days the Church shall also find refuge and consolation in faithful souls, especially in the seclusion of the religious life.

7. St. Michael, the guardian angel of the Church, shall come with his hosts to defend her against the onslaughts of Satan and his minions. The followers of St. Michael are the angelic hosts of heaven and all faithful bishops and priests of the Church. The minions of Satan are the fallen angels with the leaders of heresy, schism, and persecution.

8, 9. The battle is waged in the Church, the kingdom of heaven, from which the dragon and his angels are cast out and hurled down to earth. The earth symbolizes the nations hostile to the Church, — the world over which Satan rules. By the aid of St. Michael the Church shall purge herself of all heretics, schismatics and apostates. A similar work was accomplished by the Council of Trent in the sixteenth century.

CHAPTER XII

10. And I heard a loud voice in heaven saying: Now is come salvation, and strength, and the kingdom of our God, and the power of his Christ: because the accuser of our brethren is cast forth, who accused them before our God day and night.

11. And they overcame him by the blood of the Lamb, and by the word of the testimony, and they loved not their lives unto death.

12. Therefore rejoice, O heaven, and you that dwell therein. Woe to the earth, and to the sea, because the devil is come down unto you, having great wrath, knowing that he hath but a short time.

---

[154] See below, v. 14.

13. And when the dragon saw that he was cast unto earth, he persecuted the woman, who brought forth the man child:

14. And there was given to the woman two wings of a great eagle, that she might fly into the desert unto her place, where she is nourished for a time and times, and half a time, from the face of the serpent.

15. And the serpent cast out of his mouth after the woman, water as it were a river; that he might cause her to be carried away by the river.

16. And the earth helped the woman, and the earth opened her mouth, and swallowed up the river, which the dragon cast out of his mouth.

17. And the dragon was angry against the woman: and went to make war with the rest of her seed, who kept the commandments of God, and have the testimony of Jesus Christ.

18. And he stood upon the sands of the sea.

10, 11. St. Michael and his angels give glory to God for the victory of the Church which is achieved by the power of the Precious Blood shed for man's redemption. Satan is overcome according to Christ's testimony that "the gates of hell shall never prevail" against His Church.[155] Victory was also made possible by the invincible courage of the faithful who hesitated not to give their life in defense of the Church. Those shall be days of great persecution in which the Church will suffer all the horrors of the early ages, but she will likewise be crowned with the glory of innumerable martyrs.

12, 13. The Church is called upon to rejoice over the defeat of the dragon and the glorious martyrdom of her children; but woe to the earth and the sea, — all mankind. Realizing that the time of his power is short, Satan will now loose upon earth all his rage and fury in a last effort against the Church. His attempt to destroy her from within having failed, he will now seek to crush her by hatred and persecution from without.

14. In this new danger the Church shall receive the wings of an eagle to defend her and carry her to the place of refuge which God has prepared.[156] The wings are probably two armies sent in defense of the Church by some nation that remains faithful. This interpretation seems justified by verse 16.

In a spiritual sense the two wings are faith and prayer. In the faith and prayer of her children, and especially in the contemplative life of religious

---

[155] St. Matthew xvi, 18.

[156] See above, v. 6.

orders the Church shall find a refuse of consolation which Satan cannot violate. The desolation of those three and one-half years may be compared to that of the three days following our Lord's death on the Cross. The faith and prayers of Mary, of the holy women, and of the Apostles afforded the only consolation in those days of anguish.

This chapter indicates that the Church shall find refuge for three and one-half years on two different occasions; the one during the internal warfare against the Church and the other after the dragon has been east out. It is possible that the two-fold attack against the Church will be carried on simultaneously, making the refuge mentioned in verse 6 coincide with the one mentioned here. However, the whole context seems to be against such an interpretation.

15, 16. The dragon now seeks to overwhelm the Church with a veritable flood of tribulations, but some faithful nation, or nations, (the earth) comes to her rescue. This verse proves that the great revolt of nations mentioned by St. Paul[157] will not be universal. God will preserve at least one nation to defend the Church in that hour when, humanly speaking, everything seems hopeless.

17, 18. Satan now realizes that victory will be difficult. His first attempt failed miserably. In this second conflict new tactics must be employed. He will now seek to lead the faithful astray by a false Messias whom he will raise up in the person of Antichrist. This new adversary is to spring from the sea, — the nations already hostile to the Church, — hence Satan takes his stand by the shore to call forth the man of sin, the son of perdition.[158] It is a solemn moment of "fear and expectation of what shall come upon the whole world."[159]

---

[157] II Thessalonians ii, 3.

[158] II Thessalonians ii, 3.

[159] St. Luke xxi, 26.

THE REIGN AND CONDEMNATION OF ANTICHRIST

CHAPTER XIII

1. And I saw a beast coming up out of the sea, having seven heads and ten horns, and upon his horns ten diadems, and upon his heads names of blasphemy.

2. And the beast, which I saw, was like to a leopard, and his feet were as the feet of a bear, and his mouth as the mouth of a lion. And the dragon gave him his own strength, and great power.

3. And I saw one of his heads as it were slain to death: and his death's wound was healed. And all the earth was in admiration after the beast.

4. And they adored the dragon, which gave power to the beast, and they adored the beast, saying: Who is like to the beast? and who shall be able to fight with him?

5. And there was given to him a mouth speaking great things, and blasphemies: and power was given to him to do two and forty months.

6. And he opened his mouth unto blasphemies against God, to blaspheme his name, and his tabernacle, and them that dwell in heaven.

7. And it was given unto him to make war with the saints, and to overcome them. And power was given him over every tribe, and people, and tongue, and nation.

8. And all that dwell upon the earth adored him, whose names are not written in the book of life of the Lamb, which was slain from the beginning of the world.

9. If any man have an ear, let him hear.

10. He that shall lead into captivity, shall go into captivity: he that shall kill by the sword, must be killed by the sword. Here is the patience and the faith of the saints.

1. The beast from the sea is Antichrist who was foretold by Daniel, the prophet, in a vision quite similar to this of St. John.[160] Our study of the Apocalypse thus far makes it certain that the beast cannot be identified with the Roman Empire as many interpreters have done. Others, following

---

[160] Daniel vii, 19-22.

the opinion of St. Augustine,[161] take the beast as a symbol of all the wicked and unfaithful. This interpretation is true in a measure since Antichrist could not accomplish his nefarious work without disciples and followers. Hence the beast may be taken by extension to represent the whole empire of Antichrist. Nevertheless it is certain, in fact Suarez holds it as an article of faith, that Antichrist is a definite individual. The words of St. Paul to the Thessalonians leave no room for doubt in this matter.[162]

It is a very general opinion that Antichrist will set himself up as the Messias. This opinion seems to be supported by the words of our Savior: "I am come in the name of my Father, and you receive me not: if another shall come in his own name, him you will receive."[163] This pretension to Messiasship will make it necessary that he spring from the Jewish race.

The coming of Antichrist opens the decisive conflict between the Church and the powers of hell. It shall be the complete realization of the prophecy of Genesis: "I will put enmities between thee and the woman and thy seed and her seed."[164] The seed of the serpent is Antichrist and his followers; the seed of Mary, the woman, is Jesus Christ and his faithful disciples.

The beast has seven heads and ten horns like those of the dragon. As the representative of Satan Antichrist will be aided and abetted by the same kings and rulers symbolized in both instances by the horns and diadems. Antichrist will follow in the footsteps of his master by employing every form of sin and error to seduce the faithful.[165] Hence each head is branded with a name descriptive of the sin or error it represents. All heresies blaspheme by denying some dogma of Faith; thus, for example, atheism denies the existence of God; Arianism rejects the divinity of Christ; Mohammedanism denies both the divinity of Christ and the Trinity of God, while Judaism refuses to recognize our Lord as Messias.

2. The beast resembles a leopard in cruelty. The feet of a bear are symbols of stealth, while the mouth of a lion is an emblem of that strength and power which Satan confers upon his representative. Through the power of Satan, Antichrist will perform great wonders to deceive the people and lead them to accept him as the true Messias. St. Paul says that the coming

---

[161] St. Augustine, "City of God" xx, 19.

[162] II Thessalonians ii, 3-9.

[163] St. John V, 43; see also I John ii, 18.

[164] Genesis iii, 15.

[165] See above, page 122.

of Antichrist will be "according to the working of Satan, in all power, and signs, and lying wonders."[166] Our Lord also warns the faithful of false miracles in those days: "For there shall arise false Christs, and false prophets, and shall show signs and wonders insomuch as to deceive (if possible) even the elect. Behold I have told it to you beforehand."[167]

3, 4. The head wounded unto death but healed in a marvelous manner signifies that one of the powers supporting the cause of Antichrist shall be overcome by the sword in its conflict with the Church. But to the surprise of all, this power will quickly rally its forces and thereby lead many to believe in Antichrist.[168] As noted above, the heads represent spiritual rather than temporal powers. Since the heads of the dragon wear the diadems of royalty they may symbolize powers that combine both the spiritual and the temporal.

Those who adore Antichrist on account of his "lying wonders" thereby adore Satan who gives the power to perform them. Power and material prosperity are the rewards for those who serve him as the devil signified to Christ on the mountain: "All these (kingdoms) will I give to thee, if falling down thou wilt adore me."[169] Antichrist accepts this infamous bargain and received the empire of the world, — "Who shall be able to fight against him?"

5-8. The power of Antichrist will be of short duration (three and one-half years), but during this time he will pour out blasphemies against God and against the Blessed Sacrament of the altar (the tabernacle of God). He will also malign and vilify those who remain faithful to God and to His Church. He will be given power to wage war against the Church and to overcome it for a time. He shall rule over many nations and many peoples will adore him: his kingdom shall have the semblance of catholicity or universality. This is the great revolt of the nations foretold by St. Paul,[170] but it shall not be truly universal; one nation, at least, shall remain faithful to the Church in those days,[171] and the elect whose names are written in the book of life will not adore Antichrist.

---

[166] II Thessalonians ii, 9.

[167] St. Matthew xxiv, 24, 25.

[168] See below, on xvii, 10, 11.

[169] St. Matthew iv, 9.

[170] II Thessalonians ii, 3.

9, 10. These two verses contain consoling promises to the faithful, but dire warnings for the wicked; hence the solemn admonition: "If any one have an ear, let him hear." Antichrist and his followers, at first victorious, shall soon be overcome and destroyed. As they have meted out to others, it shall be measured unto them.[172] They who have led the faithful into captivity and put them to death, shall themselves be made captives and put to the sword. Hence the faithful must suffer in patience with full confidence of victory.

CHAPTER. XIII

11. And I saw another beast coming up out of the earth, and he had two horns, like a lamb, and he spoke as a dragon.

12. And he executed all the power of the former beast in his sight; and he caused the earth, and them that dwell therein, to adore the first beast, whose wound to death was healed.

13. And he did great signs, so that he made also fire to come down from heaven unto the earth in the sight of men.

14. And he seduced them that dwell on the earth, for the signs, which were given him to do in the sight of the beast, saying to them that dwell on the earth, that they should make the image of the beast, which had the wound by the sword, and lived.

15. And it was given him to give life to the image of the beast, and that the image of the beast should speak; and should cause, that whosoever will not adore the image of the beast, should be slain.

16. And he shall make all, both little and great, rich and poor, freemen and bondmen, to have a character in their right hand, or on their foreheads.

17. And that no man might buy or sell, but he that hath the character, or the name of the beast, or the number of his name.

18. Here is wisdom. He that hath an understanding let him count the number of the beast. For it is the number of a man: and the number of him is six hundred sixty-six.

11. The beast arising from the earth is a false prophet — the prophet of Antichrist.[173] Our divine Savior has a representative on earth in the person

---

[171] See above.

[172] St. Matthew vii, 2.

of the Pope upon whom He has conferred full powers to teach and govern. Likewise Antichrist will have his representative in the false prophet who will be endowed with the plenitude of satanic powers to deceive the nations.

If Antichrist be of Jewish extraction, as he probably will, the sea from which he arises signifies Judaism. Then the earth whence comes the second beast is a symbol of the Gentile nations in revolt against the Church. The two horns denote a twofold authority — spiritual and temporal. As indicated by the resemblance to a lamb, the prophet will probably set himself up in Rome as a sort of antipope during the vacancy of the papal throne mentioned above.[174] But the elect will not allow themselves to be deceived; they will recall the words of our Lord: "Then if any man shall say to you: Lo here is Christ, or there, do not believe him."[175]

12. Antichrist will establish himself in Jerusalem[176] where a great number of Jews will have gathered through some such movement as Zionism. The vast majority of Jews have ever clung to the belief that God will one day restore the kingdom of Israel through a Messias — an "Anointed one" — of the house of David.[177] When Antichrist manifests himself to those in Jerusalem with his "lying wonders" they will immediately proclaim him their king and Messias. Then through the power of false miracles the prophet will soon lead the Gentile nations to adore him as the true Messias promised of old by the prophets. St. Paul clearly states that Antichrist will give himself out as God: "He opposeth, and is lifted up above all that is called God, or that is worshipped, so that he sitteth in the temple of God, shewing himself as if he were God."[178]

Many theologians believe that Antichrist will rebuild the temple of Jerusalem in which he will establish his throne and be worshipped as God. The words of St. Paul, cited above, certainly seem to favor this belief, and there can be no doubt that such an achievement would secure immediate recognition for Antichrist and his projects. On the other hand the prophecy

---

[173] See below, xvi, 13; xix, 20.

[174] See above.

[175] St. Matthew xxiv, 23.

[176] Cf. xi, 8; xiv, 20; xvi, 19.

[177] Encyclopaedia Americana, Art, "Jews and Judaism — Zionism."

[178] II Thessalonians ii, 4.

of Daniel seems to preclude such a possibility: "And there shall be in the temple the abomination of desolation: and the desolation shall continue even to the consummation, and to the end."[179] It matters not how scholars interpret this abomination, the words of Christ clearly prove that it was to lead directly to the destruction of the temple by the Roman army in 70 A. D. The destruction then wrought shall be final, — it shall "continue even to the consummation, and to the end."

Julian the Apostate attempted to rebuild the temple in the fourth century but the undertaking was frustrated in a miraculous manner. "The place was made inaccessible by fearful balls of fire that broke out near the foundations and so scorched and burned the workmen that they were forced to retire. The frequent attacks finally caused the work to be abandoned."[180]

The "temple of God" in the above passage from St. Paul probably means all places of Catholic worship in general, and in particular the churches of Rome and Jerusalem. The "abomination of desolation" has been wrought in many Catholic churches by heretics and apostates who have broken altars, scattered the relics of martyrs and desecrated the Blessed Sacrament. At the time of the French Revolution a lewd woman was seated upon the altar of the cathedral in Paris and worshipped as the goddess of reason. Such things but faintly foreshadow the abominations that will desecrate churches in those sorrowful days when Antichrist will seat himself at the altar to be adored as God.

13-15. The prophet, of course, shall have power to perform the wonderful works of his master. Among other prodigies he will bring down fire from heaven, probably to offset the preaching and miracles of Elias, and thus seduce great numbers. He will also have statues of Antichrist erected to be adored by those whom he has seduced. These statues will give out oracles as did those of ancient paganism. In fact the reign of Antichrist and his prophet will be a veritable renewal of paganism throughout the world.

16. The followers of Antichrist will be marked with a character in imitation of the sign that St. John saw upon the foreheads of the servants of God.[181] This indicates that Antichrist and his prophet will introduce

[179] Daniel ix, 27; St. Matthew xxiv, 15.

[180] Ammianus Marcellinus xxiii, 1; Catholic Library, Archaeology Series, vol. iv, 153.

ceremonies to imitate the Sacraments of the Church. In fact there will be a complete organization — a church of Satan set up in opposition to the Church of Christ. Satan will assume the part of God the Father; Antichrist will be honored as Savior, and his prophet will usurp the role of Pope. Their ceremonies will counterfeit the Sacraments and their works of magic be heralded as miracles. A similar project was attempted in the fourth century when Julian the Apostate counterfeited Catholic worship with pagan ceremonies in honor of Mithras and Cybele. He established a priesthood and instituted ceremonies in imitation of Baptism and Confirmation.[182]

17. During the persecution under Diocletian statues of the gods were set up in stores and market places where customers were obliged to honor them and offer incense. None could buy or sell without the contamination of pagan worship.[183] In the days of Antichrist the false prophet will adopt similar tactics to accomplish the downfall of the faithful. No one will be able to buy or sell the necessities of life without implicating himself in the worship of Antichrist.

18. For the name of Antichrist, St. John gives a cryptogram that will enable the faithful to recognize him as soon as he makes his appearance in the world. This cryptogram consists of the numerical value of the letters in his name. St. John says that it is the number of a man. This may mean that the cryptogram is to be solved by methods in common use among men. It may also mean that the name is that of a definite individual, thus showing that Antichrist is not to be identified with the Roman Empire nor with the wicked in general as some maintain.[184]

In computing the number of Antichrist authors are divided in their opinions as to whether the Latin, Greek, or Hebrew letters should be used. The prevailing opinion today regards the use of Hebrew as the most probable. In the new Jewish kingdom of Jerusalem the use of Hebrew will certainly be encouraged if not made obligatory. Even today Hebrew is one of the recognized languages of Palestine, and is widely used by the Jews living there.

---

[181] See above.

[182] Catholic Library, Archaeology Series, vol. iv, page 148.

[183] Catholic Library, Archaeology Series, vol. iv. page 123.

[184] International Critical Commentary — Revelation of St. John, vol. i, page 364.

At present, the majority of scholars, both Catholic and Protestant, interpret the number 666 as a cryptogram for Nero Caesar as written in Hebrew characters. But according to our interpretation this is an impossible solution because the days of Antichrist are still in the future. Furthermore, the career of Nero does not correspond to that of Antichrist except in so far as he persecuted the Church. His coming was not "in all power, and signs and lying wonders" as St Paul predicts concerning Antichrist.[185]

Father Sloet of Holland proposed a solution based upon the title of Antichrist as king of Israel.[186] The Jews have ever looked forward to the Messias as a great leader to restore the kingdom of Israel. They rejected our Lord because He did not fulfill this expectation. We may be sure that the pretensions of Antichrist will not be wanting in this regard. He will be king of a restored Israel, — not only king, but the king par excellence. In Hebrew this idea could be expressed by the words hammelek l'Yisrael, which have the requisite numerical value of 666; but in order to obtain this number kaph medial must be used in melek (king) instead of kaph final.

---

[185] II Thessalonians ii, 9.

[186] Fr. Sloet in letter to Pere Gallois dated May 18, 1893.

PROPHETS OF VICTORY

CHAPTER XIV

1. And I beheld, and lo a lamb stood upon Mount Sion, and with him an hundred forty-four thousand, having his name, and the name of his Father, written on their foreheads.

2. And I heard a voice from heaven, as the noise of many waters, and as the voice of great thunder: and the voice which I heard, was as the voice of harpers, harping on their harps.

3. And they sang as it were a new canticle, before the throne, and before the four living creatures, and the ancients: and no man could say the canticle, but those hundred forty-four thousand, who were purchased from the earth.

4. These are they who were not defiled with women: for they are virgins. These follow the Lamb whithersoever he goeth. These were purchased from among men, the first fruits to God and to the Lamb.

5. And in their mouth was found no lie; for they are without spot before the throne of God.

Victory for the Church has already been foretold in connection with the account of the two witnesses;[187] but to encourage the faithful St. John once more insists upon the coming triumph in which Antichrist and his prophet shall be completely overcome and their cities destroyed.

1, 4, 5. In this vision, St. John sees a lamb standing on Mount Sion, the mystic Jerusalem, surrounded by a great throng of faithful virgins who sing His praises in a new canticle. The Lamb is Christ who ever dwells in his Church (Sion) to guard and guide it, and to receive the worship of faithful souls. The hundred forty-four thousand have been purchased from earth and become first fruits to God by vows of religious profession.

During the so-called Reformation many religious left the Church and violated their vows of chastity. No doubt still greater numbers will follow their example in the days of Antichrist, but many will remain faithful to the Church and to their vows; no lie will be found in their mouth. They will

---

[187] Cf. ch. xi.

persevere in the service of God, following the Lamb withersoever He goeth. Since first fruits were offered to God in sacrifice the Greek word for first fruits is often used in the Septuagint for "sacrifice" or "offering." Its use here may intimate that many faithful religious will become victims to God through martyrdom.

It should be noted that the hundred forty-four thousand mentioned here cannot be identified with those in chapter vii. The mystic number there represents all those from the various tribes of Israel who accept the Gospel before the time of Antichrist. They are certainly not all virgins. Moreover if St. John had wished to identify them he would have used the definite article here; the hundred forty-four thousand.

2. The music of this great throng of singers with their harps breaks upon the ears of the Apostles like the roll of thunder or the beating of waves on the shores of Patmos. It is a prayer of praise and thanksgiving offered to God in the name of the whole Church for victory over Antichrist and his kingdom. This prayer, made official by the approval of the Church, is offered in the presence of the ancients and the living creatures, — the priesthood of the Church.[188] In the voice of thunder and the roar of the waves we may see the anathemas of the Church against Antichrist and his prophet as in x, 3.

CHAPTER XIV

6. And I saw another angel flying through, the midst of heaven, having the eternal gospel, to preach unto them that sit upon the earth, and over ([189]) every nation, and tribe, and tongue and people:

7. Saying with a loud voice: Fear the Lord, and give him honor, because the hour of his judgment is come; and adore ye him, that made heaven and earth, the sea, and the fountains of waters.

8. And another angel followed, saying: That great Babylon is fallen, is fallen; which made all nations drink of the wine of the wrath of her fornication.

9. And the third angel followed them, saying with a loud voice: If any man shall adore the beast and his image, and receive his character in his forehead, or in his hand:

---

[188] See above, ch. iv, 4.

[189] This should be "to" or "unto" as in the previous phrase.

10. He also shall drink of the wine of the wrath of God, which is mingled with pure wine in the cup of his wrath, and shall be tormented with fire and brimstone in the sight of the holy angels, and in the sight of the Lamb.

11. And the smoke of their torments shall ascend up for ever and ever: neither have they rest day nor night, who have adored the beast and his image, and whosoever receiveth the character of his name.

12. Here is the patience of the saints, who keep the commandments of God, and the faith of Jesus.

13. And I heard a voice from heaven saying to me: write: Blessed are the dead, who die in the Lord. From henceforth now, saith the spirit, that they may rest from their labors; for their works follow them.

6. An angel, — great saints or apostles raised up to the Church in those days, — brings the Gospel to every nation. Despite the powers of hell it shall overcome all enemies and endure forever: it is an eternal Gospel. This is a promise of complete and final victory, — a promise made to all nations, tribes, and tongues. It shall be realized in the universal reign of Christ.[190]

7. The angel exhorts all to turn to the God of heaven and earth because the day of judgment is at hand. This is not a reference to the general judgment at the last day, but to the judgments about to fall upon Antichrist and his followers as predicted in the following verses.

8. A second angel, or apostle, announces the approaching fall of Babylon to be described in chapter xviii. Babylon is Rome, the seat of the false prophet and the capital of a neo-pagan empire. For political reasons St. John could not safely refer to Rome by name in this connection, so he uses the symbolic name as St. Peter had done before him.[191]

Under the leadership of the false prophet Rome will seduce other Gentile nations to worship Antichrist. For this infidelity she shall be destroyed. In Scripture infidelity to God is often depicted as fornication or adultery.[192]

9-11. A third angel threatens all followers of Antichrist with eternal damnation. They shall be punished with all the rigors of God's infinite justice untempered by mercy. The wine of wrath shall be poured into the

---

[190] See below, ch. xx, 1-4.

[191] I Peter v, 13.

[192] See above; cf. Cath. Library, Arch. Series vol 3, p. 2.

cup unmixed with the water of mercy. This is a reference to the ancient custom of mixing water with wine for drinking.[193]

These verses clearly prove that the pains of hell are eternal, and without respite. "The smoke of their torments shall ascend up forever and ever: neither have they rest day nor night."

12, 13. The faithful must suffer in patience, ever bearing in mind the reward that awaits them in heaven. Happy are they who die in the Lord, especially those faithful heroes who suffer even unto death for their Faith. Their works shall follow them, for their glory in heaven will be commensurate with their sufferings on earth.

CHAPTER XIV

14. And I saw, and behold a white cloud; and upon the cloud one sitting like to the Son of man, having on his head a crown of gold, and in his hand a sharp sickle.

15. And another angel came out from the temple crying with a loud voice to him that sat upon the cloud: Thrust in thy sickle, and reap, because the hour is come to reap: for the harvest of the earth is ripe.

16. And he that sat on the cloud thrust his sickle into the earth, and the earth was reaped.

17. And another angel came out of the temple which is in heaven, he also having a sharp sickle.

18. And another angel came out from the altar, who had power over fire; and he cried with a loud voice to him that had the sharp sickle, saying: Thrust in thy sharp sickle, and gather the clusters of the vine- yard of the earth; because the grapes thereof are ripe.

19. And the angel thrust in his sharp sickle into the earth, and gathered the vineyard of the earth, and cast it into the great press of the wrath of God:

20. And the press was trodden without the city, and blood came out of the press, up to the horses bridles, for a thousand and six hundred furlongs.

14-16. The followers of Antichrist have been warned of defeat and eternal punishment; the faithful have been encouraged by promise of victory here and eternal happiness hereafter. The time of judgment is at hand; the final conflict now begins. The separation of the good from the

---

[193] Cf. Isaias li, 1, 22; Jeremias xxv, 15.

bad will be still further accomplished. As on the last day, Christ sends forth His angels to gather the wheat into the barns while the cockle is being bound into bundles for the fire.[194] The gathering in of the good through martyrdom is represented as a harvest. The destruction of the wicked is depicted as the vintage of God's wrath. The realization of this judgment will be found in the complete destruction of the kingdom of Antichrist as described in subsequent chapters (xv-xix).

The reaper sitting upon a bright cloud, is an angel who comes in the name of Christ to execute His orders. Hence he bears the resemblance of Christ and is surrounded by a cloud of glory. He also wears a crown of gold, the emblem of royalty, because as representative of Christ he exercises dominion over all peoples.

The cloud of glory and the crown of royalty might lead one to accept the reaper as Christ Himself. Yet the context makes it plain that the reaper cannot be identified with Christ since he is commanded by an angel to thrust in his sickle. Furthermore, Christ has told us in the Gospel that angels shall be commissioned to separate the wheat from the cockle.[195]

17, 18. The voice from beneath the altar, commanding the vintage to be gathered is the voice of a martyr whose blood cries to heaven for vengeance.[196] This martyr who has "power over fire" is probably Elias who will destroy Antichrist by sending down fire from heaven.[197] The prophet Joel also describes the judgments of God against unholy nations as a vintage and a treading of the wine-press.[198]

19-20. The wine-press of divine wrath shall be trodden outside the city of Jerusalem.[199] Final victory over Antichrist will be won through great slaughter and bloodshed in a battle near the Holy City, perhaps in the valley of Josaphat. The prophecy of Joel may refer to this event instead of the last judgment: "Let the nations come up into the valley of Josaphat: for there I will sit to judge all nations round about. . . Nations, nations in the

---

[194] St. Matthew xiii, 30.

[195] St. Matthew xiii, 38.

[196] See above, vi, 9.

[197] See above.

[198] Joel, iii, 13.

[199] See V. 1 and xvi, 16.

valley of destruction: for the day of the Lord is near in the valley of destruction."[200]

CHAPTER XV

1. And I saw another sign in heaven, great and wonderful: seven angels having the seven last plagues. For in them is filled up the wrath of God.

2. And I saw as it were a sea of glass mingled with fire, and them that had overcome the beast, and his image, and the number of his name, standing on the sea of glass, having the harps of God:

3. And singing the canticle of Moses, the servant of God, and the canticle of the Lamb, saying: Great and wonderful are thy works, O Lord God Almighty; just and true are thy ways, O King of ages.

4. And who shall not fear thee, O Lord, and magnify thy name? For thou only art holy: for all nations shall come, and shall adore in thy sight, because thy judgments are manifest.

1. During the great conflict with Antichrist, the Church shall have power to send plagues upon his empire such as those which Moses brought down upon the Egyptians.[201] The seven angels represent the bishops and priests of the Church; and especially great saints raised up to battle against the powers of darkness. The nature of these plagues indicates that they will accompany the preaching of Elias and his companion.[202]

The seven angels receive the vials from one of the four living creatures to signify that they have a mission to preach the Gospel and condemn the wicked. The plagues which they inflict are called the last because they shall fill up the measure of God's justice against His enemies and the enemies of His Church.

2-4. The sea of crystal which St. John saw in a former vision,[203] is now mingled with fire. The light which pervades it enlightens the faithful, while the fire consumes the wicked. The vision now looks to the future when Antichrist will have been completely overcome. The victors standing upon the sea of glass chant hymns of praise and thanksgiving to God. Moses'

---

[200] Joel iii, 12, 14.

[201] Exodus viii-xii.

[202] See above, xi, 5, 6.

[203] Cf. iv, 6.

song of victory over the Egyptians[204] is well suited to the occasion, especially if he be the companion of Elias in those days.

The canticle of the Lamb is another hymn of praise to God for the triumph of Christ and His Church over all enemies.[205] The manifest judgments of God against all enemies of the Church lead to the conversion of all nations and the universal reign of Christ upon earth.

---

[204] Exodus XV, 1-19.

[205] Cf. Jeremias x, 6, 7

THE SEVEN PLAGUES

CHAPTER XV

5. And after these things I looked; and behold the temple of the tabernacle of the testimony in heaven was opened:

6. And the seven angels came out of the temple, having the seven plagues, clothed with clean and white linen, and girt about the breasts with golden girdles.

7. And one of the four living creatures gave to the seven angels seven golden vials, full of the wrath of God, who liveth for ever and ever.

8. And the temple was filled with smoke from the majesty of God, and from his power; and no man was able to enter into the temple, till the seven plagues of the seven angels were fulfilled.

5. This vision reveals to St. John the nature of the plagues to be inflicted upon the empire of Antichrist. The Church, typified by the tabernacle of the Old Law, is opened to give testimony to God.[206] The Church teaching gives testimony through the preaching of the Gospel and the power of miracles. The Church militant gives testimony by the blood of martyrs shed in her defense. Through the ministry of the seven angels Christ will condemn and punish those who refuse this twofold testimony.

6, 7. The seven angels are the ministers of the Church, and perhaps also the angelic hosts of heaven who labor in unison as the ministers of God to accomplish His decrees. They are clothed in the priestly garments of white linen, and girt about with golden cinctures, symbols of preparedness and charity.[207]

8. A cloud by day and fire by night hung over the tabernacle in the wilderness to assure the Israelites of God's protecting presence.[208] Likewise in the vision of Isaias a cloud of smoke symbolized God's special presence in the temple of Jerusalem.[209] Here the smoke filling the temple

---

[206] Exodus xl, 32.

[207] See above, i, 13.

[208] Exodus xl, 34, 35.

[209] Isaias vl, 4.

must signify that God will manifest His power in a special manner to protect the Church against the onslaughts of her enemies.

No one can enter the temple; in other words, no nation will be converted until the seven plagues have accomplished the overthrow of Antichrist and the destruction of his empire.

CHAPTER XVI

1. And I heard a great voice out of the temple, saying to the seven angels: Go, and pour out the seven vials of the wrath of God upon the earth.

2. And the first went and poured out his vial upon the earth, and there fell a sore and grievous wound upon men, who had the character of the beast; and upon them that adored the image thereof.

3. And the second angel poured out his vial upon the sea, and there came blood as it were of a dead man; and every living soul died in the sea.

4. And the third angel poured out his vial upon the rivers and the fountains of waters; and there was made blood.

5. And I heard the angel of the waters saying: Thou art just, O Lord, who art, and who wast, the Holy One, because thou hast judged these things.

6. For they have shed the blood of saints and prophets, and thou hast given them blood to drink; for they are worthy.

7. And I heard another, from the altar, saying: Yea, O Lord God Almighty, true and just are thy judgments.

1. The great voice proceeding from the temple filled with the divine presence would seem to be the voice of God Himself, but the wording of the command rather opposes this interpretation: "Pour out the vials of the wrath of God." It is probably the voice of the living creature who gave the vials to the angels, thus showing that they are commissioned by the authority of the Church.

2. The first vial is poured out upon earth to inflict malignant sores upon those who follow Antichrist. This resembles the sixth plague sent upon Egypt in which "there came boils with swelling blains in men and beasts."[210] God also threatened the unfaithful Jews in the wilderness with like punishment: "May the Lord strike thee with a very sore ulcer in the knees and in the legs, and be thou incurable from the sole of the foot to the top of

---

[210] Exodus ix, 10.

the head"[211] Herod Arippa was similarly stricken when he allowed himself to be hailed as God.[212]

In a moral sense this plague refers to the shame and confusion of those who harden their hearts and close their ears to the voice of the Church. In this sense it refers especially to the Jews who rejected the true Messias and become leaders against His Church in the days of Antichrist.

3. The second plague changes the waters of the sea into blood and destroys all living things therein. This may be taken literally as in the first Egyptian plague when Moses turned the waters of all Egypt into blood. In a figurative sense the sea represents the nations in revolt against the Church. They shall be chastised by war and revolution almost to extermination. But if the destruction of "every living soul" be taken literally the sea must refer to particular nations or peoples.

4. The streams and their sources shall likewise be changed into blood. In a symbolic meaning this signifies that the teachers of error and blasphemy shall be slain.

5, 6. The Church teaches that nations as well as individuals have angels to guide and protect them. The Bible speaks of the guardian angels of the Persians and Macedonians.[213] The angel of the waters mentioned here must be the guardian of those nations hostile to the Church. He is forced to acknowledge the justice of God's judgment against them. It is just retribution for the blood of martyrs which they have shed. What they meted out to others is now measured unto themselves.[214]

7. A voice from the altar proclaims the justice of God's dealings with those wicked nations: "Just and true are Thy judgments, Lord God Almighty." This is probably the voice of the martyrs approving the manifestations of justice for which they had prayed.[215]

CHAPTER XVI

8. *And the fourth angel poured out his vial upon the sun, and it was given unto him to afflict men with heat and fire:*

---

[211] Deuteronomy xxviii, 35.

[212] Acts of the Apostles xii, 23.

[213] Daniel x, 13; Acts of the Apostles xvi, 9.

[214] St. Matthew vii, 2.

[215] See ch. vi, 10.

9. And men were scorched with great heat, and they blasphemed the name of God, who hath power over these plagues, neither did they penance to give him glory.

10. And the fifth angel poured out his vial upon the seat of the beast; and his kingdom became dark, and they gnawed their tongues for pain.

11. And they blasphemed the God of heaven, because of their pains and wounds, and did not penance for their works.

12. And the sixth angel poured out his vial upon that great River Euphrates; and dried up the water thereof, that a way might be prepared for the kings from the rising of the sun.

13. And I saw from the mouth of the dragon, and from the mouth of the beast, and from the mouth of the false prophet, three unclean spirits like frogs.

14. For they are the spirits of devils working signs, and they go forth unto the kings of the whole earth, to gather them to battle against the great day of the Almighty God.

15. Behold, I come as a thief. Blessed is he that watcheth, and keepeth his garments, lest he walk naked, and they see his shame.

16. And he shall gather them together into a place, which in Hebrew is called Armagedon.

8, 9. The fourth vial is emptied on the sun which thereupon sends forth its scorching rays to torture the wicked; but Pharao-like instead of being converted they harden their hearts and blaspheme God.

In a figurative sense the burning rays of the sun are the rigors of God's justice. Christ, the sun of justice, is a guiding light to the faithful, but a consuming fire to the wicked.

10, 11. The fifth plague is directed against Jerusalem, the residence of Antichrist and the capital of his kingdom. This kingdom of darkness shall be made still darker by the confusion and ruin. The enemies of the Church shall bite their tongues in anger and despair, yet they will not repent of their sins.

12. As in ix, 14, the Euphrates symbolizes nations in revolt against the Church. Here they are the Gentile nations subject to Antichrist. The vision probably means that these nations shall be so reduced in strength by the sixth plague that kings from the East will not hesitate to march against them. These eastern kings probably represent nations that remain faithful to the Church and now come to her defense.[216]

13, 14. Antichrist and his prophet prepare to resist this attack by sending out messengers with the power of false miracles. By means of these prodigies kings and people are rallied to the cause of Antichrist and march to his defense against the invading armies.

15. This verse is a warning to the faithful to be prepared for the great conflict. They must guard well their garments of good works lest they be found without God's grace in that evil day. Our Lord gave a similar warning when He foretold the destruction of Jerusalem: "Watch ye therefore, because you know not what hour your Lord will come."[217]

16. The armies from the East will meet the forces of Antichrist near Jerusalem.[218] The scene of carnage that follows makes the field of battle another Mageddo, where the invading armies are completely victorious. A further description of the battle is found in ch. xix. It seems that it will occur after the fall of Rome.

Armagedon is the Greek for Har-Mageddo (Mount Mageddo), a place often drenched with Israel's blood.[219] The defeat of Antichrist may be accomplished on this very battle ground.

CHAPTER XVI

17. And the seventh angel poured out his vial upon the air, and there came a great voice out of the temple from the throne, saying: It is done.

18. And there were lightnings, and voices, and thunders, and there was a great earthquake, such an one as never had been since men were upon the earth, such an earthquake, so great.

19. And the great city was divided into three parts; and the cities of the Gentiles fell. And great Babylon came in remembrance before God, to give her the cup of the wine of the indignation of his wrath.

20. And every island flew away, and the mountains were not found.

21. And great hail, like a talent, came down from heaven upon men: and men blasphemed God for the plague of the hail: because it was exceeding great.

---

[216] See above.

[217] St. Matthew xxiv, 42.

[218] Cf. ch. xiv, 19, 20.

[219] Cf. Judges V, 19; IV Kings ix, 27; xxiii, 29; Zacharias xxi, 11.

17. As the seventh angel pours out his vial upon the air, a great voice from the temple cries out "It is done." This voice, mentioned in v. 1,[220] now proclaims the defeat of Antichrist and the destruction of his empire.

18. The lightnings flashing and the thunders rolling in heaven are symbols of divine judgments. The great earthquake is the social upheaval following the fall of Antichrist.

Perhaps the thunder and lightning, and the hail mentioned below should be taken literally like the disturbance of the elements described in Exodus: "The Lord sent thunder and hail, and lightning running along the ground: and the Lord rained hail upon the land of Egypt. And the hail and fire mixed drove on together: and it was of so great bigness, as never before was seen in the whole land of Egypt."[221]

19. The great city (Jerusalem) is divided into three sections by yawning chasms caused by the earthquake. A similar punishment befell Jerusalem after the death of the two witnesses when one-tenth of the city was destroyed and seven thousand persons perished. The rending of the rocks by an earthquake at the time of our Lord's death upon the cross warrants the belief that these later disturbances will be actual upheavals of the earth.

In a figurative sense the division of the city may refer to rival factions warring amongst themselves. During the siege of Jerusalem by the Roman army in 70 A. D. the greatest sufferings were caused by warring factions within the walls of the city.[222]

Rome, the great Babylon, is also destroyed and the cities of the Gentiles are laid waste. These cities are probably the capitals of those nations that submit to the domination of the neo-pagan empire of Rome and thus become parts of the empire of Antichrist.

20, 21. The severity of divine judgments against all unfaithful nations is graphically portrayed by the symbolic expressions of these verses. The destruction of the ancient Roman empire is described in almost identical language.[223]

---

[220] Cf. also ch. xxi, 3.

[221] Exodus ix, 23, 24; cf. Josue x, 11.

[222] Josephus, "Wars of the Jews," Book V.

[223] Ch. vi, 14, 15; cf. also Isaias xiii; Ezechiel x, xxii; Joel ii.

THE BEAST AND THE HARLOT

CHAPTER XVII

1. And there came one of the seven angels, who had the seven vials, and spoke with me, saying: Come, I will show thee the condemnation of the great harlot, who sitteth upon many waters,

2. With whom the kings of the earth have committed fornication; and they who inhabit the earth, have been made drunk with the wine of her whoredom.

3. And he took me away in spirit into the desert. And I saw a woman sitting upon a scarlet colored beast, full of names of blasphemy, having seven heads and ten horns.

4. And the woman was clothed round about with purple and scarlet, and gilt with gold, and precious stones and pearls, having a golden cup in her hand, full of the abomination and filthiness of her fornication.

5. And on her forehead a name was written: a mystery; Babylon the great, the mother of the fornications, and the abominations of the earth.

6. And I saw the woman drunk with the blood of the saints, and with the blood of the martyrs of Jesus. And I wondered, when I had seen her, with great admiration.

7. And the angel said to me: Why dost thou wonder? I will tell thee the mystery of the woman, and of the beast which carrieth her, which hath the seven heads and ten horns.

8. The beast which thou sawest, was, and is not, and shall come up out of the bottomless pit, and go into destruction: and the inhabitants on the earth (whose names are not written in the book of life from the foundation of the world) shall wonder, seeing the beast that was, and is not.

9. And here is the understanding that hath wisdom. The seven heads are seven mountains, upon which the woman sitteth, and they are seven kings:

10. Five are fallen, one is, and the other is not yet come: and when he is come, he must remain a short time.

11. And the beast which was, and is not: the same also is the eighth, and is of the seven, and goeth into destruction:

12. And the ten horns which thou sawest, are ten kings, who have not yet received a kingdom, but shall receive power as kings one hour after the beast.

13. These have one design: and their strength and power they shall deliver to the beast.

14. These shall fight with the Lamb, and the Lamb shall overcome them, because he is Lord of lords, and King of kings, and they that are with him are called, and elect, and faithful.

15. And he said to me: The waters which thou sawest, where the harlot sitteth, are peoples, and nations, and tongues.

16. And the ten horns which thou sawest in the beast: these shall hate the harlot, and shall make her desolate, and naked, and shall eat her flesh, and shall burn her with fire.

17. For God hath given into their hearts to do that which pleaseth him, that they give their kingdom to the beast till the words of God be fulfilled.

18. And the woman which thou sawest, is the great city, which hath kingdom over the kings of the earth.

1, 2. The fall and devastation of Rome were mentioned in the preceding chapter,[224] but its importance as the seat of the false prophet and the capital of a worldwide empire under Antichrist demands a more detailed account. Hence St. John now describes at length the new pagan empire of Rome (ch. xvii), and foretells its complete and final destruction (ch. xviii).

The great harlot sitting by many waters is Rome holding sway over many nations[225] that share in her corruption and infidelity to God. Ancient Tyre and Ninive were likewise designated as harlots by the prophets Isaias and Nahum.[226] St. John simply follows out the symbolism in which infidelity to God is called fornication and adultery.[227]

3. St. John is led into a desert which foreshadows the great devastation and desolation that shall be wrought upon the unfaithful city. There he beholds a harlot seated upon a scarlet beast having seven heads and ten horns and covered over with names of blasphemy. This is evidently the beast from the sea, — a symbol of Antichrist.[228] Hence the vision indicates

---

[224] Ch. xvi, 19; cf. also ch, xiv, 8.

[225] See below, v. 15.

[226] Isaias xxiii, 16, 17; Nahum iii, 4.

[227] See above.

that the new pagan empire of Rome holds sway over the nations through the power and influence of Antichrist.

Scarlet is the emblem of imperial power, — a power exercised over the nations by Antichrist through his prophet in Rome. Scarlet is also the color of blood and forebodes terrible persecutions in which the blood of martyrs will flow in copious streams. The significance of the heads and horns and the names of blasphemy has been explained in connection with the beast from the sea.[229] A further development is found in verses 9, 17.

4. The harlot wears a mantle of purple and gold, an emblem of the imperial power possessed by Rome as capital of a vast empire. The gems and golden cup imply riches and material prosperity, but the cup is filled with every iniquity and immorality.[230] Riches and luxury have ever been the great demoralizers of nations as well as of individuals.

5. Through her power and riches Rome leads other nations to worship Antichrist and imitate her own immoralities. Hence the harlot bears upon her forehead the mystic title: "Babylon the Great, Mother of the Fornications and the Abominations of the Earth." It seems that Roman harlots often wore upon their foreheads a label whereon their names were conspicuously displayed.[231] Here the name is a mystery showing that Babylon is used figuratively for Rome as in the Epistle of St. Peter and other early literature.[232]

6, 7. The woman glutted with the blood of martyrs is a warning to the faithful of great persecutions at Rome and throughout the empire during the reign of Antichrist and his prophet.

8-11. The angel's interpretation bristles with difficulties. He says the beast was, and is not, but shall come forth from the abyss only to perish again after a short time. In verse 11 the beast is identified with one of the heads which shall be the eighth although it is one of the seven, and shall quickly go into destruction. Further on (v. 16), it is said that the ten horns of the beast (in Greek, "the ten horns and the beast") will fight against the harlot and destroy her by fire.

---

[228] See ch. xiii, 1.

[229] See above.

[230] Jeremias li, 7; Ezechiel xxviii, 13-19.

[231] Seneca, "Controv. i."

[232] I Peter iv, 13; Sibylline Oracles v, 143, 159; II Baruch lxvii, 7.

Those who take Nero to be the Antichrist find an explanation for these mysteries, which at first sight, seems quite plausible. They have recourse to a popular legend that Nero, after attempting suicide, fled to the East and would soon reappear with the Parthian armies to conquer Rome and regain his throne.[233] The writing of the Apocalypse is assigned to the reign of Vespasian who thus becomes the sixth head, — the one who "now is," — Titus is the seventh who is yet to come. His short reign fulfills the prediction: "He must remain a short time." Then Nero, one of the five who have fallen, returns with the kings of Parthia (the ten horns) to regain his throne and establish himself as the eighth although he is one of the seven.

This interpretation is ingenious but impossible because, as already noted, Nero cannot be identified with Antichrist.[234] But the insuperable difficulty lies in the fact that it destroys inspiration. The use of a legend in an inspired work might be admitted, incongruous though it seems, but a prophecy without fulfillment cannot be inspired. Yet according to the above widely received interpretation the prophecy remains unfulfilled except in so far as Domitian was known as a second Nero on account of his cruelty.[235] If the ten horns be interpreted as the Parthian kings, or satraps, there is no ground in history for representing Domitian or any other Emperor, as their leader. Neither was Rome ever destroyed by a Parthian invasion.

The settled conviction of many scholars that Nero was Antichrist makes it necessary to refer this whole prophecy to the time of St. John and interpret the seven heads as Roman Emperors. But the context shows that the prophecy concerns events that are still in the future, and most probably the seven kings will not be emperors of Rome. The "one who now is" refers not to the time of St. John, but to the time when the prophecy shall be fulfilled.

St. John says there will be many Antichrists; in fact there were many even in his day: "Even now there are become many Antichrists; whereby we know that it is the last hour."[236] Again he writes: "And every spirit that dissolveth Jesus is not of God: and this is Antichrist of whom you have heard that he cometh and he is now already in the world."[237] According to

---

[233] Tacitus, "Histories" ii, 8; Suetonius, "Nero" 57.

[234] See above.

[235] Cf. Juvenal iv, 37 sq.; Martial xi, 33; Tertullian, Apology v.

[236] I John ii, 18.

these words of St. John every teacher of error and every adversary of the Church is an Antichrist.

Nero has ever been considered one of the principal Antichrists. Sts. Peter and Paul were the two witnesses raised up against him. Arius, leader of the first great heresy may well be called an Antichrist with St. Athanasius and St. Hilary as the witnesses opposed to him. Mahomed, Luther, and Voltaire are often enumerated as Antichrists and many others could be added to the list.

These few examples are sufficient to show that Antichrist will be like the true Messias in having forerunners who typify him in various ways; and since they are types of Antichrist it is not surprising that the prophecies concerning him can often be applied to them also in one or more particulars. But in Antichrist alone will they be realized in every particular. Hence the faithful will recognize him and avoid his snares, but the rest of mankind will be deceived by his "lying wonders."

The angel tells St. John that the seven heads are seven mountains and seven kings. The seven mountains upon which the harlot sits are quite generally interpreted as the seven hills of Rome. The only apparent reason for mentioning the seven hills would be to show that the name Babylon is used figuratively for Rome, but the usage seems to have been well known to the early Christians. The connection of kings and mountains under one symbol suggests the imagery of the ancient prophecies where mountains so often figure as symbols of kingdoms and empires.[238] Hence the seven heads, which are seven mountains, may be the seven principal nations subject to Rome in the days of Antichrist.

One of the seven kings devotes himself and his kingdom so completely to the cause of Antichrist that he can rightly be identified with the beast as is done in verse 11. This is the head which St. John saw in a former vision where it was wounded unto death but revived and healed in a mysterious manner to the astonishment of all.

"Five are fallen, one is, and the other is not yet come," and the "beast which was, and is not; the same also is the eighth, and is of the seven, and goeth into destruction." Any attempt to explain this mysterious prophecy before its accomplishment can be nothing more than speculation. Nevertheless we may find a solution that has some degree of probability.

---

[237] I John iv, 3.

[238] Cf. Isaias xli, 15; Jeremias ii, 25; Daniel II, 35, 44; Zacharias iv, 7.

Verse 10 may mean that five nations supporting the cause of Antichrist are overcome, one still maintains the conflict, and a seventh has not yet submitted to the domination of Rome, but will soon do so only to be defeated after a short time. Through the influence of Antichrist and his lying wonders, the nation most devoted to his cause will rally from defeat and be organized anew as the eighth kingdom although it is really one of the seven. It shall soon go down to destruction in the final defeat of Antichrist and the destruction of his empire.

Again the prophecy may be interpreted of the rulers instead of their kingdoms. In this sense "five are fallen," etc., would probably mean that the rulers of five nations have fallen from power, presumably by violent means, but the sixth still holds his throne. In the seventh kingdom a ruler is yet to come who will use his power in support of Antichrist.

One of the five kings, identified with the beast on account of his great devotion to the cause of Antichrist, has received a sword wound unto death[239] but is quickly healed and reorganizes his kingdom, or obtains power over another nation. Thus he becomes the eighth, yet in reality he is one of the seven. The sword wound unto death may be understood literally thus making this extraordinary recovery one of the "lying wonders" of Antichrist, or his prophet, to deceive the nations.

12-14. The ten horns are ten kings or princes who shall come to the assistance of Antichrist for a short time.[240] They will place all their power and resources at his command to accomplish the one object in view, — the destruction of the Church. Despite their efforts they shall be overcome by the faithful of Christ who is Lord of lords and King of kings.

15. As in other visions the waters, or the sea, symbolize human society. Here they represent in particular the peoples and nations subject to Rome and with her in revolt against the Church. The seven principal ones were symbolized above by seven mountains.

16, 17. After a time the beast and his allied kings (the ten horns) will make war upon Rome and lay it waste with fire and sword. The barbarian invasions of Rome in the fourth and fifth centuries give some idea of the manner in which Rome shall become the prey of a "scourge of God"[241] in punishment for revolt against the Church and for its worship of Antichrist.

---

[239] Cf. xiii, 3, 14.

[240] The Greek text reads "one hour with the beast"; cf. also above.

[241] Attila called himself the "scourge of God."

St. John gives no reason why Antichrist and his allies turn against Rome except that God puts it into their hearts to accomplish His purposes.

According to the Vulgate, only the ten kings will make war upon Rome: "The ten horns which thou sawest in the beast: these shall hate the harlot," etc. The Greek text reads: "The ten horns which thou sawest and the beast: these shall hate," etc. This is evidently the better reading, as it fits into the context. God put it into the hearts of the ten kings to give their power to the beast to do His words. The "Swords of God" can be nothing else than the destruction of Rome.

THE FALL OF BABYLON

CHAPTER XVIII

1. And after these things, I saw another angel come down from heaven, having great power; and the earth was enlightened with his glory.

2. And he cried out with a strong voice, saying: Babylon the great is fallen, is fallen; and is become the habitation of devils, and the hold of every unclean spirit, and the hold of every unclean and hateful bird:

3. Because all nations have drunk of the wine of the wrath of her fornication; and the kings of the earth have committed fornication with her; and the merchants of the earth have been made rich by the power of her delicacies.

4. And I heard another voice from heaven, saying: Go out from her, my people; that you be not partakers of her sins, and that you receive not of her plagues.

5. For her sins have reached unto heaven, and the Lord hath remembered her iniquities.

6. Render to her as she also hath rendered to you; and double unto her double according to her works: in the cup wherein she hath mingled, mingle ye double unto her.

7. As much as she hath glorified herself, and lived in delicacies, so much torment and sorrow give ye to her; because she saith in her heart: I sit a queen, and am no widow; and sorrow I shall not see.

8. Therefore shall her plagues come in one day, death, and mourning, and famine, and she shall be burned with fire; because God is strong, who shall judge her.

9. And the kings of the earth, who have committed fornication, and lived in delicacies with her, shall weep, and bewail themselves over her, when they shall see the smoke of her burning.

10. Standing afar off for fear of her torments, saying: Alas, alas! that great city Babylon, that mighty city: for in one hour is thy judgment come.

11. And the merchants of the earth shall weep, and mourn over her: for no man shall buy their merchandise any more.

12. Merchandise of gold and silver, and precious stones; and of pearls, and fine linen, and purple, and silk, and scarlet, and all thyine wood, and all manner of vessels of ivory, and all manner of vessels of precious stones, and of brass, and of iron, and of marble.

13. And cinnamon, and odors, and ointment, and frankincense, and wine, and oil, and fine flour, and wheat, and beasts, and sheep, and horses, and chariots, and slaves, and souls of men.

14. And the fruits of the desire of thy soul are departed from thee, and all fat and goodly things are perished from thee, and they shall find them no more at all.

15. The merchants of these things, who were made rich, shall stand afar off from her, for fear of her torments, weeping and mourning,

16. And saying: Alas! alas! that great city, which was clothed with fine linen, and purple, and scarlet, and was gilt with gold, and precious stones, and pearls.

17. For in one hour are so great riches come to nought; and every shipmaster, and all that sail into the lake, and mariners, and as many as work in the sea, stood afar off,

18. And cried, seeing the place of her burning, saying: What city is like to this great city?

19. And they cast dust upon their heads, and cried, weeping and mourning, saying: Alas! alas! that great city, wherein all were made rich, that had ships at sea, by reason of her prices: for in one hour she is made desolate.

20. Rejoice over her, thou heaven, and ye holy apostles and prophets; for God hath judged your judgment on her.

21. And a mighty angel took up a stone, as it were a great millstone, and cast it into the sea, saying: With such violence as this shall Babylon, that great city, be thrown down, and shall be found no more at all.

22. And the voice of harpers, and of musicians, and of them that play on the pipe, and on the trumpet, shall no more be heard at all in thee; and no craftsman of any art whatsoever shall be found any more at all in thee; and the sound of the mill shall be heard no more at all in thee;

23. And the light of the lamp shall shine no more at all in thee; and the voice of the bridegroom and the bride shall be heard no more at all in thee: for thy merchants were the great men of the earth, for all nations have been deceived by thy enchantments.

24. And in her was found the blood of prophets and of saints, and of all that were slain upon the earth.

1, 2. The mighty angel is probably a great saint or prophet raised up to enlighten the Church by his teaching and to foretell the destruction of Rome as Jonas foretold the fall of Ninive, and Daniel that of ancient Babylon. But if "angel" be taken literally it is probably St. Michael, the guardian of the Church or St. Gabriel, the mighty one of God.

The angel speaks of the fall of Rome as something already accomplished to show that it must surely come to pass. It shall be left so desolate that wild beasts will find it a fitting abode and unclean birds will hover about its ruins. Thus also did Isaias prophesy concerning ancient Babylon: "Wild beasts shall rest there and their houses shall be filled with serpents . . . and owls shall answer one another there, in the houses thereof, and sirens in the temples of pleasure."[242]

Some interpreters take the words of the angel to mean that the ruins of Rome shall become the lurking place of evil spirits according to the words of Christ: "When an unclean spirit is gone out of a man he walketh through dry places seeking rest."[243]

3. The terrible destruction and desolation of Rome is a punishment for her many sins and for the sins into which she has led other nations. The kings and merchants of the earth have been led into the sins and vices of Rome, and with her they have upheld Antichrist in his efforts against the Church.

4, 5. Another voice from heaven, — a voice of mercy, — warns the faithful of the impending ruin and exhorts them to seek safety in flight. In like manner did our Lord warn His disciples to flee from Jerusalem upon the approach of the Roman army.[244] Heeding these words of warning the faithful fled to Pella in Peraea and thus escaped the terrible sufferings of the siege.

6-8. These verses are an apostrophe to the ministers of God's judgments, apparently the ten kings of the preceding chapter. They are to punish the wicked and unfaithful city for all the evils she has heaped upon them, presumably the evils resulting from apostasy and adherence to Antichrist. They shall punish her also for her own apostasy and worship of Antichrist: "Double unto her double according to her works: in the cup wherein she hath mingled mingle ye double unto her."

---

[242] Isaias xiii, 21, 22.

[243] St. Matthew xii, 43.

[244] St. Matthew xxiv, 16-8.

The ruin and desolation of Rome shall be commensurate with her former glory, riches and power. The proud city that "sits a queen" with neither fear nor anxiety, shall be humbled in the dust.

9, 10. The kings of earth who have shared her guilt shall lament the fate of the city, but they stand afar off fearing to come to her assistance. Such is usually the friendship between nations!

11-16. The merchants of the earth "who were made rich, shall stand ajar off from her for fear of her torments, weeping and mourning, and saying: Alas! alas! that great city, which was clothed with fine linen, and purple, and scarlet, and was gilt with gold and precious stones, and pearls. For in one hour are so great riches come to nought."

17-19. In like manner do they who have prospered in the sea commerce with Rome bewail the loss of their markets: "Alas! alas! that great city wherein all were made rich that had ships at sea by reason of her prices; for in one hour she is made desolate."

20. The Apostles and prophets and all saints are called upon to rejoice at this manifestation of God's justice. The prayers of the martyrs[245] are answered and their blood requited. The mention of Apostles may refer especially to Sts. Peter and Paul who suffered martyrdom at Rome under Nero.

21-24. These verses complete the picture of desolation brought upon the rich and powerful city. She shall be destroyed to remain forever but a heap of ruins because through her have all nations been deceived "and in her is found the blood of prophets and of saints, and of all that were slain upon the earth." The blood of martyrs throughout the empire is justly chargeable to Rome from which went forth the decrees of persecution.

---

[245] Ch. vi, 10.

THE HYMN OF VICTORY

CHAPTER XIX

1. After these things I heard as it were the voice of much people in heaven, saying: Alleluia. Salvation, and glory, and power is to our God.

2. For true and just are his judgments, who hath judged the great harlot which corrupted the earth with her fornication, and hath revenged the blood of his servants at her hands.

3. And again they said: Alleluia. And her smoke ascendeth for ever and ever.

4. And the four and twenty ancients, and the four living creatures fell down and adored God that sitteth upon the throne, saying: Amen; Alleluia.

5. And a voice came out from the throne, saying: Give praise to our God, all ye his servants; and you that fear him, little and great.

6. And I heard as it were the voice of a great multitude, and as the voice of many waters, and as the voice of great thunders, saying, Alleluia: for the Lord our God the Almighty hath reigned.

7. Let us be glad and rejoice, and give glory to him; for the marriage of the Lamb is come, and his wife hath prepared herself.

8. And it is granted to her that she should clothe herself with fine linen, glittering and white. For the fine linen are the justifications of saints.

9. And he said to me: Write: Blessed are they that are called to the marriage supper of the Lamb. And he saith to me: These words of God are true.

10. And I fell down before his feet, to adore him. And he saith to me: See thou do it not: I am thy fellow servant, and of thy brethren, who have the testimony of Jesus. Adore God. For the testimony of Jesus is the spirit of prophecy.

1-3. In response to the summons given above (xviii, 20), St. John hears the voices of praise from great multitudes. They arc the martyrs in heaven and the faithful on earth singing the praises of God for the manifestation of His justice in the fall of Rome. The ruins of the city shall remain as a lasting memorial of God's judgments upon unfaithful nations and peoples: "Her smoke ascendeth for ever and ever."

4-6. The four and twenty ancients and the four living creatures, — the entire priesthood of the Church, — prostrate themselves in adoration and chant the words of praise: "Amen, Allelujah." A voice from the throne invites all servants of God to praise and adore Him, whereupon a mighty chorus goes up from the elect: "Allelujah, for the Lord our God the Almighty hath triumphed and now reigns over all nations." The united voices of this mighty throng resound like the roll of thunder or the beating of waves.

7, 8. They rejoice because the marriage of the Lamb is at hand and His spouse is in readiness. The Church, the spouse of Christ, ever triumphant in heaven, now triumphs on earth. She is clothed in radiant garments which are the good works of her faithful children.

9. The angel, — the voice from the throne, — commands St. John to write: "Blessed are they who are called to the marriage supper of the Lamb." This marriage feast, or triumph of the Church, begins on earth but is consummated only in heaven. In this connection St. Gregory the Great remarks that as supper is taken before the night's repose so the supper of the Lamb precedes the repose of eternal happiness in heaven.[246] The marriage supper is also a symbol of the Holy Eucharist to which all the faithful are invited, and in which they receive a foretaste of eternal union with Christ in heaven.

10. Filled with joy the aged Apostle falls at the feet of the angel to adore him, evidently mistaking him for our Lord. But the angel restrains him with the words; "See thou do it not for I am only thy fellow servant, like unto others who have received the spirit of prophecy to give testimony to Jesus."[247]

CHAPTER XIX

11. And I saw heaven opened, and behold a white horse; and he that sat upon him was called faithful and true, and with justice doth he judge and fight.

12. And his eyes were as a flame of fire, and on his head were many diadems, and he had a name written, which no man knoweth but himself.

13. And he was clothed with a garment sprinkled with blood, and his name is called, The Word of God.

---

[246] St. Gregory the Great, "Homil. in Evang." ii, 24.

[247] Cf . also ch. xxii, 8, 9.

14. And the armies that are in heaven followed him on white horses, clothed in fine linen, white and clean.

15. And out of his mouth proceedeth a sharp two-edged sword; that with it he may strike the nations. And he shall rule them with a rod of iron; and he treadeth the wine press of the fierceness of the wrath of God the Almighty.

16. And he hath on his garment, and on his thigh written: King of Kings, and Lord of Lords.

11. Our Lord Himself now appears as a conqueror upon a white horse.[248] Christ possesses all perfections, but in the triumph of the Church, fidelity to His promise that the gates of hell should never prevail against her, stands out most prominent. Hence He is called the Faithful and True One.

12. As in a former vision, His eyes are like flames of fire.[249] The many diadems signify that Christ, the King of kings, is master of all nations. The name which no man knoweth expresses some perfection or attribute of our Savior not yet made known to the world. It probably has some connection with the universal reign of the Church after Antichrist.

13, 14. The blood-stained garment may mean that victory for the Church was won through the merits of Christ and His martyrs as stated in xii, 11: "And they overcame him by the blood of the Lamb . . . and they loved not their lives unto death." The blood may also be that of the enemies of Christ and His Church as is intimated by the treading of the winepress of God's anger (v. 15). This recalls the words of Isaias: "I have trodden the winepress alone ... I have trampled on them in my indignation, and have trodden them down in my wrath, and their blood is sprinkled upon my garments, and I have stained all my apparel."[250]

Our Lord is followed by an army of the faithful upon white horses, symbols of victory. They are the "called and elect and faithful," mentioned in the preceding chapter, who fight with the Lamb against the ten kings.[251] They are probably the armies of faithful nations symbolized in xii, 16, by the earth that helps the woman, and mentioned in xvi, 12, as kings from the rising sun.

---

[248] See above.

[249] See above.

[250] Isaias lxiii, 3.

[251] Ch, xvii, 14.

15, 16. The two-edged sword is here the sword of divine justice which strikes down unfaithful nations which Christ shall rule with a rod of iron. He treadeth the winepress of God's wrath by executing the divine decrees against all nations in revolt against God and His Church. Neither the name given to Christ here, nor the one found in verse 13, is to be identified with the unknown name mentioned in verse 12.

CHAPTER XIX

17. And I saw an angel standing in the sun, and he cried with a loud voice, saying to all the birds that did fly through the midst of heaven: Come, gather yourselves together to the great supper of God:

18. That you may eat the flesh of kings, and the flesh of tribunes, and the flesh of mighty men, and the flesh of horses, and of them that sit on them, and the flesh of all freemen and bondmen, and of little and of great.

19. And I saw the beast, and the kings of earth, and their armies gathered together to make war with him that sat upon the horse, and with his army.

20. And the beast was taken, and with him the false prophet who wrought signs before him wherewith he seduced them who received the character of the beast, and who adored his image. These two were cast alive into the pool of fire, burning with brimstone.

21. And the rest were slain with the sword of him that sitteth upon the horse, which proceedeth out of his mouth; and all the birds were filled with their flesh.

17, 18. While Rome, the seat of the false prophet, is smouldering in ashes, Christ and His faithful followers go forth to give battle against Antichrist and his allied kings. An angel summons all birds of prey to feast upon the carcasses of kings and princes, freemen and bondmen, great and small for the slaughter shall be great.[252]

19, 20. Antichrist and his allied kings now make a last effort against the forces of Christ and His Church. "I saw the beast and the kings of earth and their armies gathered together to make war with him that sat upon the horse." This seems to be a reference to the battle at Armagedon mentioned above (xvi, 16). Three false prophets were sent out as messengers of Antichrist to gather the kings of earth to battle but Antichrist and his forces

---

[252] Ezechiel xxxix, 17-20; Jeremias xii, 9.

are overcome and a voice from the temple cries out "It is done." Antichrist and his prophet are cast into hell, and their allies put to the sword. It is the last battle in the great conflict between the Church and the powers of darkness.

PART III: From the Closing of the Abyss to the End of the World

And I saw an angel coming down from heaven, having the keg to the bottomless pit, and a great chain in his hand. And he laid hold on the dragon, the old serpent, which is the devil and satan, and hound him for a thousand gears.

APOCALYPSE
xx, i, 2.

THE UNIVERSAL REIGN OF JESUS CHRIST

CHAPTER XX

The words of St. Paul to the Thessalonians[253] prove clearly that Antichrist must be a definite individual, and our study of the Apocalypse shows that he has not yet made his appearance in the world. But practically all interpreters who accept these conclusions take the reign of Antichrist as a prelude to the last judgment and the end of the world. Then, contrary to the plain sense of Holy Scripture, they place the universal reign of Christ before the time of Antichrist. This, in turn, makes the chaining of the dragon a difficult problem. Some refer it to the time of our Savior's death, or to the day of Pentecost. Others fix upon the date of Constantine 's conversion, the reign of Charlemagne, the fall of the Western Empire, or the capture of Constantinople by the Turks, — all purely arbitrary dates as their great divergencies prove.

A careful reading of the Apocalypse shows clearly that Antichrist will appear long centuries before the last judgment and the end of the world. In fact his reign will be but the final attempt of Satan to prevent the universal reign of Christ in the world. Since the day of Pentecost the Church has been engaged in perpetual warfare. Judaism was her first enemy; then followed Arianism, Mohammedanism, the Greek Schism, the Reformation, and secret societies fostering atheism and rationalism. Today she is also battling against indifferentism and a recrudescence of paganism. The reign of Antichrist shall be the final conflict in this prolonged struggle with the powers of darkness.

After the defeat of Antichrist the Gentile nations will return to the Church and the Jews will enter her fold. Then shall be fulfilled the words of Christ: "There shall be one fold and one shepherd."[254] Unfortunately sin and evil will not have entirely disappeared, the good and the bad will still be mingled in the Church, although the good shall predominate. After many centuries, symbolized by a thousand years, faith will diminish and charity grow cold as a result of the long peace and security enjoyed by the

---

[253] II Thessalonians ii, 8.

[254] St. John X, 16.

Church. Then Satan, unchained for a short time, will seduce many nations (Gog and Magog) to make war on the Church and persecute the faithful. These apostate nations shall be promptly overwhelmed with a deluge of fire and the Church will come forth again triumphant. The general judgment and the end of the world will then be near at hand. Men will be living in daily expectation until our Lord appears in the clouds with the suddenness of a lightning flash.[255] Then shall all people be gathered together unto judgment.

The establishment of the Church over all nations is foretold on almost every page of Holy Scripture. "He shall rule from sea to sea and from the river unto the ends of the earth. . . . And all kings of the earth shall adore him; and all nations shall serve him."[256] "All the nations thou has made shall come and adore before thee, Lord."[257] "His empire shall be multiplied and there shall be no end of peace."[258] "His kingdom is an everlasting kingdom, and all kings shall serve him and obey him."[259] "He shall speak peace to the Gentiles, and his power shall be from sea to sea, and from the rivers even to the ends of the earth."[260]

The Apostles were sent forth to preach the Gospel to all nations and to every creature,[261] and St. Paul applies to them the words of the Psalmist: "Their sound hath gone forth into all the earth, and their words unto the end of the whole world."[262] Can it be supposed that these prophecies are fulfilled by the conversion of a few thousand souls in the various pagan countries of the world? Can we admit that a world steeped in paganism, and torn with schism and heresy is the only result of Christ's death upon the Cross? Such an admission is necessary if the closing of the abyss and the binding of Satan be placed at the beginning of Christianity, and the thousand years of Christ's reign, before the defeat of Antichrist.

---

[255] St. Matthew xxiv, ,2.7.

[256] Ps. lxxi, 8, 9.

[257] Ps. lxxxv, 9.

[258] Isaias ix, 7.

[259] Daniel vii, 27.

[260] Zacharias ix, 10.

[261] St. Matthew xxviii, 16; St. Luke xvi, 15.

[262] Romans x, 18; Ps. xviii, 5.

The prophecies cited above and hundreds of others scattered through the Scriptures make it certain that the reign of Christ shall be truly universal. After the Gentile nations return to the Faith, the Jews shall also submit to the yoke of the Gospel. St. Paul states this fact very plainly: "Blindness in part has happened in Israel, until the fulness of the Gentiles should come in." And so all Israel shall be saved as it is written: "There shall come out of Sion, he that shall deliver, and shall turn away ungodliness from Jacob."[263] Again he writes: "If the loss of them (the Jews) be the reconciliation of the world, what shall the receiving of them be, but life from the dead?"[264]

These prophecies will not be fulfilled before the time of Antichrist, since the Apocalypse clearly shows that he will come into a world harassed by paganism, apostasy, schism, and heresy."[265] The Jews still unconverted, will accept him as Messias and assist in his warfare against the Church. Only after the defeat of Antichrist and the return of the Gentile nations to the Faith, will the Jews accept Christ as the true Messias. Then shall begin the universal reign of Christ over all peoples, and tribes, and tongues.

After the destruction of Rome in the days of Antichrist, it shall remain forever but a heap of ruins, and the haunt of filthy animals; "that great city shall be found no more at all." This fact taken in connection with the many prophecies concerning the future glory of Jerusalem, justifies the belief that it will become the city of the Popes and the capital of Christendom from the time of Antichrist until the consummation of the world. This, we believe, is not opposed to the teaching of the Church. Many theologians hold that the Papacy is connected with the bishopric of Rome by divine institution; yet this cannot be an article of Faith because it is contained neither in Scripture nor in tradition. It is of faith that the successor of St. Peter is head of the Church, and in the present order of things it is also of faith that the bishop of Rome is the successor of St. Peter.[266]

Transfer of the Papacy from Rome to Jerusalem might be made by decree of a general council acting with the Pope, or by direct intervention of divine Providence. The prophets of old foretell the future glory of Jerusalem when it shall become again the Holy City and the spiritual capital of the world whence the waters of salvation flow out to all peoples.

---

[263] Romans xi, 25, 26; Isaias lix, 20.

[264] Romans xi, 15.

[265] Apocalypse ix, 20, 21.

[266] Tanquery, "Synopsis Theol. Dogm." pp. 383-4.

It shall also become the capital of a Jewish nation gathered about it once more. A few texts will suffice to establish these points.

"Rejoice and praise, O thou habitation of Sion: for great is he that is in the midst of thee, the Holy One of Israel."[267]

"Sing praise, and rejoice, daughter of Sion: for behold I come and I will dwell in the midst of thee: saith the Lord. And many nations shall be joined to the Lord in that day, and they shall be my people, and I will dwell in the midst of thee."[268]

"And there shall be one day, which is known to the Lord. . . . And it shall come to pass in that day that living waters shall go out from Jerusalem: half of them to the east sea, and half of them to the last sea; they shall be in summer and winter. And the Lord shall be King over all the earth: in that day there shall be one Lord, and His name shall be one . . . and there shall be no more anathema; but Jerusalem shall sit secure."[269]

"At that time Jerusalem shall be called the throne of the Lord: and all the nations shall be gathered together to it, in the name of the Lord of Jerusalem, and they shall not! walk after the perversity of their most wicked heart."[270]

"Thus saith the Lord of hosts: I am returned to Sion, and I will dwell in the midst of Jerusalem: and Jerusalem shall be called the city of truth, and the mountain of the Lord of hosts. . . . Behold I will save my people from the land of the east, and from the land of the going down of the sun. And I will bring them, and they shall dwell in the midst of Jerusalem: and they shall be my people, and I will be their God in truth and in justice. . . . And it shall come to pass, that as you were a curse among the Gentiles, house of Juda, and house of Israel: so will I save you, and you shall be a blessing."[271]

These and similar prophecies aroused in the Jewish breast an anxious longing for the glorious awakening of Israel. The people looked forward to the long expected Messias as a great leader of the restoration. The Apostles shared this expectation of their countrymen. When our Lord told them the Holy Ghost was shortly to come upon them they said: "Lord, wilt thou at this time restore again the kingdom to Israel?" Christ did not tell them their

---

[267] Isaias xii, 6.

[268] Zacharias ii, 10, 12.

[269] Zacharias xiv, 7-11.

[270] Jeremias iii, 17.

[271] Zacharias viii, 3, 7, 8, 13.

expectations were vain; He simply said: "It is not for you to know the times or moments which the Father has put in his own power."[272] He told them, in effect, that the kingdom would be restored to Israel but it was not for them to know the time because the Father had not revealed it.

CHAPTER XX

1. And I saw an angel coming down from heaven, having the key of the bottomless pit, and a great chain in his hand:

2. And he laid hold on the dragon, the old serpent, which is the devil and Satan, and bound him for a thousand years.

3. And he cast him into the bottomless pit, and shut him up, and set a seal upon him, that he should no more seduce the nations, till the thousand years be finished. And after that he must be loosed a little time.

4. And I saw seats; and they sat upon them; and judgment was given unto them; and the souls of them, that were beheaded for the testimony of Jesus, and

for the word of God, and who had not adored the beast nor his image, nor received his character on their forehead, or in their hands; and they lived and reigned with Christ a thousand years.

5. The rest of the dead lived not, till the thousand years were finished. This is the first resurrection.

6. Blessed and holy is he that hath part in the first resurrection. In these the second death hath no power; but they shall be priests of God and of Christ; and shall reign with him a thousand years.

1-3. Chapters ix-xix form an important part of the Apocalypse containing, as they do, an extended history of Antichrist and his warfare against the Church. As a preparation for his coming, the star fallen from heaven opens the abyss whence comes forth a great swarm of locusts.[273] Then follows a prophetic account of his reign, the overthrow of his empire, and his final condemnation in hell. An angel from heaven now binds the dragon and casts him into the abyss which is closed and sealed that Satan may no longer seduce the nations as in the past. Thus all obstacles are removed and the Church begins her peaceful reign on earth. It should be noted, however, that not all evil spirits are thus sealed up in the abyss;

---

[272] Acts of the Apostles i, 2.

[273] Ch. ix, 2, 3.

there will still be sin and evil on earth. The individual must still struggle against temptation and seduction. In fact there can be no real progress in virtue without temptation.

4. St. John now sees the souls of those who participate with Christ in the government of His Church. They are the saints who worshipped not the beast nor his image, nor received his character on their forehead, and especially they are the martyrs who gave their lives "for the testimony of Jesus and for the word of God." "Judgment was given unto them," for as St. Paul says; "the saints shall judge this world."[274] The saints and martyrs are models and patrons for the faithful whom they teach and guide by the example of their lives on earth and by their intercession in heaven. Thus do they live and reign with Christ.

5. The wicked, — the rest of the dead, — live not the life of the soul because they have been condemned to the eternal torments of hell, which is the second death because it follows the death of the body.

6. The reign of the saints and martyrs with Christ in heaven is called the first resurrection. The resurrection of the body at the last judgment shall be the second. Blessed are they who have part in the first resurrection because the second death hath no power over them.

---

[274] I Corinthians vi, 2.

LOOSING OF SATAN AND LAST PERSECUTION

CHAPTER XX

7. And when the thousand years shall be finished, Satan shall be loosed out of his prison, and shall go forth, and seduce the nations, which are over the four quarters of the earth, Gog and Magog, and shall gather them together to battle, the number of whom is as the sands of the sea.

8. And they came upon the breadth of the earth, and encompassed the camp of the saints, and the beloved city.

9. And there came down fire from God out of heaven, and devoured them; and the devil, who seduced them, was cast into the pool of fire and brimstone, where both the beast

10. And the false prophet shall be tormented day and night for ever and ever.

7, 8. At the close of the period, symbolized by a thousand years, Satan will be loosed again for a short time during which he will seduce many nations. From the four quarters of the earth he will assemble an army, numerous as the sands of the sea, to war against the Church, — the camp of the saints. Jerusalem the beloved, then the city of the Popes, will be the chief point of attack; but God will intervene in its defense by raining down fire upon the besieging hosts.

9. These hostile nations are symbolized as Gog and Magog,[275] — names made famous by the prophecy of Ezechiel in which their invasion and terrible destruction by fire is described at length. "Thou shalt come out of thy place from the northern parts, thou and many people with thee, all of them riding upon horses, a great company and a mighty army. And thou shalt come upon my people of Israel like a cloud to cover the earth. . . . And I will judge him with pestilence, and with blood, and with violent rain, and vast hailstones: and I will rain fire and brimstone upon him, and upon his army, and upon the many nations that are with him. . . And I will send fire on Magog, and on them that dwell confidently in the islands: and they shall know that I am the Lord. . . . Behold it cometh, and it is done, saith

---

[275] In Ezechiel Magog seems to be a people and Gog their ruler.

the Lord God: this is the day whereof I have spoken. . . And it shall come to pass in that day, that I will give Gog a noted place for a sepulcher in Israel: the valley of the passengers on the east of the sea, which shall cause astonishment in them that pass by: and there shall they bury Gog and all his multitude, and it shall be called the valley of the multitude of Gog. And the house of Israel shall bury them for seven months to cleanse the land. And all the people of the land shall bury him, and it shall be unto them a noted day, wherein I was glorified, saith the Lord God."[276]

10. Satan is now east into hell to be tormented with the beast and the false prophet for all eternity.

---

[276] Ezechiel xxxviii, xxxix.

RESURRECTION AND GENERAL JUDGMENT

CHAPTER XX

11. And I saw a great white throne, and one sitting upon it, from whose face the earth and heaven fled away, and there was no place found for them.

12. And I saw the dead great and small, standing in the presence of the throne, and the books were opened; and another book was opened, which is the book of life; and the dead were judged by those things which were written in the books according; to their works.

13. And the sea gave up the dead that were in it, and death and hell gave up their dead that were in them; and they were judged every one according to their works.

14. And hell and death were cast into the pool of fire. This is the second death.

15. And whosoever was not found written in the book of life was cast into the pool of fire.

11. St. John now beholds our Lord seated upon His throne to judge the living and the dead. Heaven and earth fleeing before His face expresses the terror that shall seize upon the wicked: "Men withering away for fear and expectation of what shall come upon the whole world. For the powers of heaven shall be moved."[277]

Our Lord's coming with power and majesty, and the signs that precede it were not revealed to St. John, probably because they had been sufficiently announced by Christ Himself in the Gospels.[278]

12. "Wheresoever the body shall be, there shall the eagles also be gathered together."[279] In like manner at the coming of Christ the dead arise and come to judgment. The books are now opened and all are judged according to their works which are written either in the book of life or in

---

[277] St. Luke xxi, 26.

[278] St. Matthew xxiv, sq.; St. Mark xiii, 22 sq.; St. Luke xxi, 25 sq.

[279] St. Matthew xxiv, 28.

the books of the dead. The books of the dead (wicked) are many while there is but one book of life because "many are called but few are chosen."[280]

13. The sea represents the nations opposed to the Church in the last days. Its dead are the people of those nations whom Christ shall, find living at His coming. They are dead in sin and their works are written in the books of the dead.

Death and hell must give up their dead, — the wicked who die before the second coming of Christ. Their souls, condemned to hell, are now united to their risen bodies to appear before the judgment seat of Christ. Thus do death and hell give up their dead.

14, 15. Those whose names are not written in the book of life are condemned, body and soul, to eternal torments which is the second death. Hence death and hell (the wicked) are cast into the pool of fire to be tormented for ever with the beast and his prophet.

The order of events immediately preceding the last judgment can be fairly well established from various passages of Scriptures. The revolt of Gog and Magog will be punished by a deluge of fire from heaven which will probably occasion the conversion of great numbers. At some time after this the signs foreboding the coming of Christ will strike terror into all hearts,[281] and the day of judgment will be near at hand. "When these things begin to come to pass, look up, and lift up your heads, because your redemption is at hand."[282] "But of the day and hour no one knoweth, no not the angels of heaven, but the Father alone."[283] St. Paul says that the "day of the Lord shall come as a thief in the night"; men will be found in the midst of their occupations as happened at the deluge of the days of Noe.[284]

At length there "shall appear the sign of the Son of man in heaven; and then shall all tribes of earth mourn: and they shall see the Son of man coming in the clouds with much power and majesty. And He shall send His angels with a trumpet and a great voice, and they shall gather together His elect from the four winds of heaven, from the farthest parts of the heaven to the utmost bounds of them."[285] At the sound of the trumpet the dead

---

[280] St. Matthew xxii, 14.

[281] St. Matthew xxiv, 29; St. Mark xiii, 24; St. Luke xxi, 25.

[282] St. Luke xxi, 28.

[283] St. Matthew xxiv, 36.

[284] I Thessalonians v, 2; St. Matthew xxiv, 37.

shall arise. The just found living upon earth in that day and the just who arise from the dead shall be caught up into the air to meet Christ and be united with Him forever. "The dead who are with Christ shall arise first. Then we who are alive, who are left shall be taken up together with them in the clouds to meet Christ into the air and so shall we be always with the Lord."[286]

The wicked still living on earth and those raised up from the dead shall also be brought to judgment. Both good and bad are judged according to their works; "they that have done good things shall come forth unto the resurrection of life," and shall hear those words of Christ: "Come ye blessed of my Father, possess you the kingdom prepared for you from the foundation of the world."[287] But they that have done evil shall hear those words of eternal judgment: "Depart from me, ye cursed, into everlasting fire which was prepared for the devil and his angels."[288]

The words of St. Paul, "the dead who are with Christ shall rise first," do not mean that the resurrection of the just will take place before that of the wicked. St. Paul was writing to correct the erroneous belief of the Thessalonians that the just who are alive at the second coming of Christ will enjoy the glories of heaven sooner than those who have died. He tells them that the dead shall arise and then all shall be taken up together to meet Christ. Hence "we who are alive, who remain unto the coming of the Lord shall not be before them who have slept."[289]

Shall those found living at the second coming of Christ undergo death before the judgment? The Church has decided nothing in the matter, but Sacred Scripture seems to indicate that they will not. St. Paul says: "We who are alive shall be taken up." Again he says: "In a moment, in the twinkling of an eye, at the sound of the last trumpet . . . the dead shall arise again incorruptible; and we shall be changed."[290] He evidently makes a distinction between those who are dead and those who remain alive at the coming of Christ. In the preceding verse the Apostle writes: "We shall all

---

[285] St. Matthew xxiv, 31.

[286] I Thessalonians iv, 15, 16.

[287] St. John V, 29; St. Matthew xxv, 34.

[288] St. John V, 29; St. Matthew xxv, 41.

[289] I Thessalonians iv, 14.

[290] I Corinthians xv, 52; cf. also II Corinthians v, 4, 5.

indeed rise again; but we shall not all be changed." This indicates that all must undergo death but the Greek text reads: "We shall not all sleep, but we shall all be changed." It must be admitted that this reading agrees better with the context than the one found in the Vulgate.

However the question is of little importance. We must all be changed; "this corruptible must put on incorruption; and this mortal must put on immortality."[291] The bodies of the just will be spiritualized and glorified as was the body of our divine Savior: "it is sown a natural body, it shall rise a spiritual body; it is sown in dishonor, it shall rise in glory.[292] Now it matters little indeed whether this change be accomplished directly in the living body or indirectly by death and immediate resurrection.

---

[291] I Corinthians xv, 53.

[292] I Corinthians xv, 43, 44.

THE HEAVENLY JERUSALEM

CHAPTER XXI

1. And I saw a new heaven and a new earth, for the first heaven and the first earth was gone, and the sea is now no more.

2. And I John saw the holy city, the new Jerusalem, coming down out of heaven from God, prepared as a bride adorned for her husband.

3. And I heard a great voice from the throne, saying: Behold the tabernacle of God with men, and he will dwell with them. And they shall be his people; and God himself with them shall be their God.

4. And God shall wipe away all tears from their eyes; and death shall be no more, nor mourning, nor crying, nor sorrow shall be any more, for the former things are passed away.

5. And he that sat on the throne, said: Behold I make all things anew. And he said to me: Write, for these words are most faithful and true.

6. And he said to me: It is done. I am Alpha and Omega; the beginning and the end. To him that thirsteth, I will give of the fountain of the water of life, freely.

7. He that shall overcome shall possess these things, and I will be his God; and he shall be my son.

8. But the fearful, and the unbelieving, and the abominable, and murderers, and whoremongers, and sorcerers, and idolaters, and all liars, they shall have their portion in the pool burning with fire and brimstone, which is the second death.

1-4. A former vision revealed to St. John the destruction of the present world by a return to chaos as at the beginning of creation.[293] This destruction will be accomplished by fire as St. Peter distinctly states: "But the heavens and the earth which now are, by the same word are kept in store, reserved unto fire against the day of judgment and perdition of the ungodly men. . . . But the day of the Lord shall come as a thief, in which the heavens shall pass away with great violence, and the elements shall be melted with heat, and the earth and the works which are in it, shall be burnt

---

[293] See above.

up."[294] Out of the elements thus purified by fire, God will form a new, — a glorified earth to be a suitable habitation for the glorified bodies of the just. Then will the Church triumphant, — the new Jerusalem, — descend upon earth to be the tabernacle of God with men. They shall be his people and He will be their God. They shall be happy with Him forever; "death shall be no more, nor mourning, nor crying, nor sorrow shall be any more, for the former things are passed away."

The renewal of the earth completes the "restitution of all things" mentioned by St. Peter.[295] It is the revelation for which all nature groaneth and travaileth in expectation, waiting for the adoption of the sons of God.[296] Isaias also prophesied this renewal: "For as the new heavens and the new earth, which I will make to stand before me, saith the Lord: so shall your seed stand and your name."[297] Hence St. Peter writes: "But we look for new heavens and a new earth according to his promises, in which justice dwelleth."[298] The "heavens" in this connection probably refers to the space occupied by the atmosphere surrounding the earth. This was the opinion of St. Augustine and St. Thomas Aquinas. Others believe that it includes all the heavenly bodies, — the entire universe. The "sea" may be taken literally, though in a symbolic sense it refers to the nations opposed to the Church.[299]

5, 6. The work of Redemption is now completed even for inanimate nature which had been cursed in the sin of man: "For the creature was made subject to vanity, not willingly, but by reason of him who made it subject in hope. Because the creature also itself shall be delivered from the servitude of corruption into the liberty of the glory of the children of God."[300]

All things began in Christ by creation; they now find their destiny in Him who is "Alpha and Omega, the beginning and the end."[301] He now gives to

---

[294] II Peter iii, 7-10.

[295] Acts of the Apostles iii, 21.

[296] Romans viii, 20-23.

[297] Isaias lxvi, 22.

[298] II Peter iii, 13.

[299] Cf. Schneider-Thurston, "The Other Life" ch. xiii, where this whole subject is discussed at length.

[300] Romans viii, 20, 21.

[301] See above.

His faithful the waters of eternal life, — the life of union with Him in the Beatific Vision.

7, 8. Eternal happiness is for those alone who overcome in the conflict with temptation and sin. All others shall suffer the eternal torments of hell which is the second death.

CHAPTER XXI

9. And there came one of the seven angels, who had the vials full of the seven last plagues, and spoke with me, saying: Come, and I will shew thee the bride, the wife of the Lamb.

10. And he took me in spirit to a great and high mountain: and he shewed me the holy city Jerusalem coming down out of heaven from God.

11. Having the glory of God, and the light thereof was like to a precious stone, as to the jasper stone, even as crystal.

12. And it had a wall, great and high, having twelve gates, and in the gates twelve angels, and names written thereon, which are the names of the twelve tribes of the children of Israel.

13. On the east, three gates; and on the north, three gates; and on the south, three gates; and on the west, three gates.

14. And the wall of the city had twelve foundations, and in them, the twelve names of the twelve apostles of the Lamb.

15. And he that spoke with me, had a measure of a reed of gold, to measure the city and the gates thereof and the wall.

16. And the city lieth in a foursquare, and the length thereof is as great as the breadth: and he measured the city with the golden reed for twelve thousand furlongs, and the length and the height and the breadth thereof are equal.

17. And he measured the wall thereof an hundred forty-four cubits, the measure of a man, which is of an angel.

18. And the building of the wall thereof was of jasper stone: but the city itself pure gold like to clear glass.

19. And the foundations of the wall of the city were adorned with all manner of precious stones. The first foundation was jasper; the second, sapphire; the third, a chalcedony; the fourth, an emerald:

20. The fifth, sardonyx: the sixth, sardius: the seventh, chrysolite, the eighth, beryl, the ninth, a topaz: the tenth, a chrysoprasus: the eleventh, a jacinth: the twelfth an amethyst.

2il. And the twelve gates are twelve pearls, one to each: and every several gate was of one several pearl. And the street of the city was pure gold, as it were transparent glass.

22. And I saw no temple therein. For the Lord God Almighty is the temple thereof, and the Lamb.

23. And the city hath no need of the sun, nor moon, to shine in it. For the glory of God hath enlightened it and the Lamb is the lamp thereof.

24. And the nations shall walk in the light of it: and the kings of the earth shall bring their glory and honor into it.

25. And the gates thereof shall not be shut by day: for there shall be no night there.

26. And they shall bring the glory and honor of the nations into it.

27. There shall not enter into it anything defiled, or that worketh abomination or maketh a lie, but they that are written in the book of life of the Lamb.

9, 10. One of the seven angels who poured out the vials of wrath, takes St. John in spirit upon a high mountain that he may have a bird's eye view, as it were, of the new Jerusalem, coming down from heaven, all ablaze with divine splendors. The great dimensions of the city are also indicated by the necessity of viewing it from a lofty mountain.

11. The glory of God enlightens the city whose radiant beauty is compared to the flashing hues of jasper, and the transparent brilliancy of crystal.

12, 13. The strong towering walls are an assurance that no enemy can assail its inhabitants nor disturb the peace and happiness that reigns within. The twelve gates inscribed with the names of the twelve tribes signify that many from each tribe shall be saved,[302] and through these tribes shall the nations be blessed.[303] Hence there are three gates on each side to show that all nations are called to the Faith and to salvation.

14. The twelve foundation stones bear the names of the twelve Apostles because Christ "built upon the foundation of the apostles and prophets, Jesus Christ Himself being the chief corner-stone, in whom all the building being framed together groweth up into an holy temple in the Lord."[304]

---

[302] See above.

[303] Genesis xxii, 18; xxvi, 4.

[304] Ephesians ii, 20, 21.

15, 16. The angel measures the city and finds that it is a cube, a symbol of perfection. The dimensions are composed of the mystic numbers 12 and 1000, symbols of perfection and immensity. The reed is of gold, the symbol of charity, to signify that none can enter the heavenly Jerusalem unless he be enriched with good works and bear the treasure of Christian charity.

17. The height of the outer wall surrounding the city is insignificant when compared to the height of the city which is perfectly secure in itself and needs no protecting wall. The wall is measured in cubits, a measure in common use among men, but now employed by the angel in a mystic sense.

18-21. The description of the mystic Jerusalem is evidently symbolic. The dimensions signify perfection and immensity; the gold and precious stones remind us that it is necessary to have the gold of true charity and the gems of virtues and good works. Thus only can we enter this city of gleaming gold and sparkling gems.

Despairing of putting into words this the most sublime part of his vision, and wishing to depict it in consonance with our understanding, St. John has recourse to the harmonious proportions of numbers, and the varied and delicate tints of precious gems. Until we see heaven and are bathed in the full light of God, we shall never discover all that the Apostle desired to convey thereby; but while here below, nothing gives us a loftier notion of heaven's blessedness than beholding St. John, the most enlightened and inspired of sacred writers, utterly powerless to express in human language the delights it holds in store for us."[305] We can only say with St. Paul: "Eye hath not seen, nor ear heard, neither hath it entered into the heart of man, what things God hath prepared for them that love Him."[306]

22, 23. No temple is found in the heavenly city because God and the Lamb are themselves the temple. There every soul is united to God and flooded with the light of His eternal glory which renders useless all created light.

24-27. The elect of all nations shall dwell in this "light inaccessible"[307] and the kings of earth shall bring thither their glory and honor to lay them before the throne of God. The gates of the city are not closed at night like

---

[305] Fouard, "St. John" (Eng. Trans.), page 130.

[306] I Corinthians ii, 9; cf. also Isaias lxiv, 4.

[307] I Timothy vi, 16.

those of earthly cities, because "night shall be no more." Only those who are pure of heart, whose names are written in the book of life, can enter through these gates.

CHAPTER XXII

1. And he shewed me a river of water of life, clear as crystal, proceeding from the throne of God and of the Lamb.

2. In the midst of the street thereof, and on both sides of the river, was the tree of life, bearing twelve fruits, yielding its fruits every month, and the leaves of the tree were for the healing of the nations.

3. And there shall be no curse any more; but the throne of God and of the Lamb shall be in it, and his servants shall serve him.

4. And they shall see his face: and his name shall be on their foreheads.

5. And night shall be no more: and they shall not need the light of the lamp, nor the light of the sun, because the Lord God shall enlighten them, and they shall reign for ever and ever.

1. The river flowing from the throne of God symbolizes the joy and happiness that floods the souls of the elect in their possession of God and union with Him.

This is the living water promised by our Lord: "He that shall drink of the water that I will give him, shall not thirst for ever: but the water that I will give him, shall become in him a fountain of water springing up into everlasting life."[308]

2. The tree of life stands in the midst of the city on either banks of the river at the disposal of all and to all it gives eternal life. Its twelve fruits ripening every month symbolize the happiness of heaven which shall be without interruption for all eternity. In this life the fruit of the tree is the Holy Eucharist, and its leaves the teachings of Christ and His Church. In heaven the fruit is the glory of the Beatific Vision; and the leaves, the accidental glory of the saints.[309]

3-5. Sin shall be no more, and the saints shall serve and glorify God whom they behold face to face. "We see now through a glass in a dark manner; but then face to face. Now I know in part; but then I shall know even as I am known."[310] The name of God written upon the foreheads of

---

[308] St. John iv, 13, 14; Psalm xxxv, 9, 10.

[309] Cath. Encyc, vol. viii, p. 174.

the saints is a mark of their adoption as children of God by Baptism and Confirmation. "Behold what manner of charity the Father hath bestowed upon us, that we should be called, and should be the sons of God."[311]

Night shall be no more; the saints need not the lamp of faith nor the guiding light of the Church. God Himself will be their light and they will reign with Him for ever. "Blessed are they that dwell in Thy house, Lord: they shall praise Thee for ever and ever."[312]

---

[310] I Corinth, xiii, 12.

[311] I John iii, 1.

[312] Psalm lxxxiii, 5

THE EPILOGUE

Behold I come quickly. Blessed is he that keepeth the words of the prophecy of this book.

APOCALYPSE
xxii 7

THE EPILOGUE

CHAPER XXII

6. And he said to me: These words are most faithful and true. And the Lord God of the spirits of the prophets sent his angel to shew his servants the things which must be done shortly.

7. And, Behold I come quickly. Blessed is he that keepeth the words of the prophecy of this book.

8. And I, John, who have heard and seen these things. And after I had heard and seen, I fell down to adore before the feet of the angel, who shewed me these things.

9. And he said to me: See thou do it not: for I am thy fellow servant, and of thy brethren the prophets, and of them that keep the words of the prophecy of this book. Adore God.

10. And he saith to me: Seal not the words of the prophecy of this book: for the time is at hand.

11. He that hurteth, let him hurt still: and he that is filthy, let him be filthy still: and he that is just, let him be justified still: and he that is holy let him be sanctified still.

12. Behold, I come quickly; and my reward is with me, to render to every man according to his works.

13. I am Alpha and Omega, the first and the last, the beginning and the end.

14. Blessed are they that wash their robes in the blood of the Lamb: that they may have a right to the tree of life, and may enter in by the gates into the city.

15. Without are dogs, and sorcerers, and unchaste, and murderers, and servers of idols, and every one that loveth and maketh a lie.

16. I Jesus have sent my angel, to testify to you these things in the churches. I am the root and stock of David, the bright and morning star.

6, 7. The angel who acted as guide for St. John in viewing the new Jerusalem, now assures him that these visions are true revelations of what the future holds in store for the Church. They are true because God Himself has revealed them to St. John through the ministry of the angel. In a former vision God commanded St. John to write "for these words are most faithful and true."[313] Their accomplishment is near at hand, for has not our Lord said: "Behold, I come quickly. Blessed is he that keepeth the words of the prophecy of this book"? The same warning is found in the opening words of the Apocalypse: "Blessed is he that readeth, and heareth the words of this prophecy; and keepeth those things which are written in it; for the time is at hand"; their fulfillment was beginning already in the days of St. John.[314]

8, 9. Probably many of these visions were not committed to writing until St. John had returned to Ephesus where he could dictate them to his disciples as was the custom of the other Apostles. Hence he is careful to attest their authenticity: "I, John, am he who saw and heard these things." Perhaps he wrote these words with his own hand as a sort of signature after the manner of St. Paul in his first Epistle to the Corinthians.[315]

When the visions and revelations were ended, St. John prostrated himself before the angel as a parting salutation, but the angel refused this mark of respect, because as prophets of God they were equals. The words of the angel imply that he is the same one whom St. John mistook for our Lord on a former occasion.[316] There St. John intended divine worship as indicated by the Greek construction. Here, there can be no mistake; St. John is well aware that his guide is one of the seven angels who poured out the vials of wrath.[317] This difference is reflected in the use of a Greek construction often found in the Old Testament to express the honor paid to angels and persons of superior rank.

10. St. John is commanded not to seal the book of his prophecy; it is to be published to the Church at once because the time for its fulfillment has already begun.[318]

11-13. Christ Himself now utters words of warning and encouragement. The wicked may continue in their evils, heaping sin upon sin, but they must know that God will deal with them according to their works. On the

---

[313] Ch. xxi, 5.

[314] Ch. i, 3.

[315] I Corinthians xvi, 21.

[316] Ch. xix, 10.

[317] Ch. xxi, 9.

[318] Ch. x, 4.

other hand, let the just be still more justified; let him add good works unto good works for he shall be rewarded accordingly. It is I, the Alpha and Omega, the first and the last, the beginning and the end, who shall punish and reward all men in justice according to their works.

14, 15. Blessed, therefore, are they who have washed their robes in the blood of the Lamb through Baptism, Penance, and martyrdom, for they shall enter the heavenly Jerusalem and be nourished by the tree of life. But woe to the wicked (dogs) who must remain without where there shall be "weeping and gnashing of teeth".[319] They shall have no part in the tree of life for Christ has said: "Give not that which is holy to dogs."[320]

16. Our Lord Himself now confirms the truth of the revelations made to His Apostles: It is I, Jesus, Who sent My angel to testify these things to the churches; I Who am the root and stock of David, the bright and morning star.[321]

CHAPTER XXII

17. And the spirit and the bride say: Come. And he that heareth, let him say; Come. And he that thirsteth, let him come: and he that will, let him take the water of life freely.

18. For I testify to every one that heareth the words of the prophecy of this book: If any man shall add to these things, God shall add unto him the plagues written in this book.

19. And if any man shall take away from the words of the book of this prophecy, God shall take away his part out of the book of life, and out of the holy city, and from these things that are written in this book.

20. He that giveth testimony of these things, saith, Surely I come quickly: Amen. Come, Lord Jessu.

21. The grace of our Lord Jesus Christ be with you all. Amen.

17. St. John, speaking in his own name, says that the Church, the bride of Christ, guided by the Holy Ghost, longs for the glorious coming of her divine Spouse. May all who hear her voice join in the self-same prayer. May those who thirst for the water of life receive it abundantly!

---

[319] St. Luke xiii, 28.

[320] St. Matthew vii, 6.

[321] See above.

18, 19. The Apostle was aware of the risks his book would run at the hands of heretics who infested the churches of Asia Minor. He had been a witness to their shrewdness in interpolating and falsifying the most sacred texts. Hence he threatens with anathema anyone who may presume to mutilate his prophecies in any manner. This warning should be extended to the entire Scriptures of which the Apocalypse is but the final chapter.[322]

20. Our Lord, who testifies to the truth of these prophecies, says: "Behold, I come quickly." From hearts filled with faith and love we cry out: "So be it. Come Lord Jesus!"

Meditation upon the prophecies of the Apocalypse should strengthen our faith in God, and increase our zeal for His holy Church. They predict the great persecution of Antichrist whose near approach is foreshadowed by many signs; yet we know that the Church will at length triumph over the powers of hell and reign peacefully over all nations. Through prayers and good works we can beseech the mercy of God to shorten those days of trial for the sake of the elect.[323] May He hasten the coming of His Kingdom! "Thy kingdom come; Thy will be done on earth as it is in heaven."

---

[322] Fouard, "St. John" (Eng. Trans.), p. 134.

[323] St. Matthew xxiv, 22.

Made in United States
Orlando, FL
15 January 2022